LEARNING FROM LEADERS:

WELFARE REFORM POLITICS AND POLICY IN FIVE MIDWESTERN STATES

Edited by
Carol S. Weissert

The
Rockefeller
Institute
Press

Rockefeller Institute Press, Albany, New York 12203-1003
© 2000 by the Rockefeller Institute Press
All rights reserved. First edition 2000
Printed in the United States of America

The Rockefeller Institute Press
The Nelson A. Rockefeller Institute of Government
411 State Street
Albany, New York 12203-1003

Library of Congress Cataloguing-in-Publication Data

Learning from leaders : welfare reform politics and policy in five midwestern states /
edited by Carol S. Weissert.
      p. cm.
   Includes bibliographical references and index.
   ISBN 0-914341-67-5 -- ISBN 0-914341-68-5 (pbk.)
     1. Public welfare--Middle West--Case studies. 2. Welfare
recipients--Employment--Middle West--Case studies. 3. Middle West--Social
policy--Case studies. 4. Middle West--Politics and government--Case studies. I.
Weissert, Carol S.

   HV98.M63 L43 2000
   361.977--dc21
                                                                99-086401

   ISBN: 0-914341-67-5 Cloth
          0-914341- 68-5 Paper

Table of Contents

Acknowledgments

This book and the field research on which the chapters are based were supported by a grant to the Nelson A. Rockefeller Institute of Government from the W. K. Kellogg Foundation as part of Foundation's Devolution Initiative. The Initiative was launched in 1996 to understand the impact of devolution and create an information base useful to a broad group of stakeholders; share findings about the effects of devolution with policymakers and the public; and use the information produced by researchers to help promote public participation. The special interest of the Kellogg Foundation in midwestern states fits nicely with the recent history of welfare reforms, which have tended to occur earlier and more extensively in that region. Thus, this book.

We at the Institute would especially like to thank C. Patrick Babcock of the W. K. Kellogg Foundation for coming up with the idea for this volume. Each of the authors of the case studies relied heavily on the willingness of many state and local officials to discuss how they were reorganizing their social service systems at the very time they were in the middle of the task. We greatly appreciate their kind cooperation. We would also like to thank Sandra Hackman for editorial assistance and Michael Cooper, director of the Institute's publications department, for shepherding this volume through its many stages to this point.

Chapter 1

LEARNING FROM MIDWESTERN LEADERS

Carol S. Weissert

Few, if any, intergovernmental programs in recent memory have received the academic, political, and public attention of the 1996 federal Personal Responsibility and Work Opportunity Reconciliation Act (PRWORA), which abolished Aid to Families with Dependent Children (AFDC) and replaced it with Temporary Assistance for Needy Families (TANF). The 1996 legislation, which converted welfare from an entitlement program administered by the states to block grants that states can use as they see fit, has led to intense media attention and legislative debate, as well as numerous studies and information sources.[1]

State welfare reform efforts that both preceded and emanated from the 1996 federal law are difficult to encapsulate in any one report or study. The difficulty lies partly in the fact that welfare reform encompasses economic and administrative dilemmas at the national, state, and local levels, and also affects recipients in myriad ways. Many state welfare programs incorporate both conservative and liberal ideas and centralize some functions while dispersing others to local control. In so doing, they reflect the federal legislation that helped shape — if not spawn — much of the state action.

One way to capture the nuances of some of this complexity — and thus to better understand the nature and potential outcomes of the experiment on which the nation has embarked—is to focus on a few key states. That is what this book does. The authors take a close

1

look at the political forces propelling welfare reform in Kansas, Michigan, Minnesota, Ohio, and Wisconsin. They examine why the states enacted the laws they did, how they delegated responsibility to state agencies, local governments, and the private and nonprofit sectors, and what those choices have meant for states' ability to track and report the outcomes of their experiments.

The authors in this book are state researchers in the State Capacity Study sponsored by The Nelson A. Rockefeller Institute of Government at the State University of New York, Albany, and funded by the W. K. Kellogg Foundation and others. Their work was part of a research project that examined how 20 states have implemented the new welfare reform programs (Nathan and Gais 1998). The research was conducted in 1997 and updated for this volume. It is based on interviews with political and administrative leaders in state and local governments, review of state documents, contracts, reports, press releases, and other relevant information on welfare reform, and detailed case studies of two local sites within each state.

Why the Midwest?

The story of welfare reform in the Midwest is significant because several governors in the region played visible and apparently influential roles in the federal debate preceding passage of PRWORA in 1996. Among the most the visible and vocal were two rather unlikely media darlings — Wisconsin Governor Tommy Thompson and Michigan Governor John Engler. Both had already prompted their states to change welfare assistance, and both strongly urged Congress to allow states to shift even more dramatically from providing cash benefits to insisting that participants find jobs (Weissert and Schram 1996, Weaver 1996).

The two governors competed mightily for press attention and bragging rights regarding welfare reform. Governor Thompson's reforms started earlier (he was elected four years before Engler), but Michigan's comprehensive state welfare reform law was enacted prior to Wisconsin's. Wisconsin and Michigan were the first and second states to submit their TANF plans to Washington. But the significance of welfare reform in these states extends far beyond competition for bragging rights. The reforms were meaningful as well as early. And they were and are useful to other states and to researchers interested in welfare policy.

Other Midwestern governors also emphasized changing the focus of welfare to emphasize work first. More quietly, but no less successfully, governors in Ohio and Minnesota built welfare systems different from those in Michigan and Wisconsin that fit the structure and politics of their own states. The governor of Kansas took a backseat on reform by eschewing the legislative arena but nevertheless shaped in quiet ways a significant welfare reform effort.

	Population 1996	Per Capita Income 1996	Unemployment 1996	AFDC Average Monthly Payment per Family 1995
Kansas	2.6 million	$23,281	4.5	$336
Michigan	9.6 million	$24,810	4.9	$414
Minnesota	4.7 million	$25,580	4.0	$520
Ohio	11.2 million	$23,537	4.9	$310
Wisconsin	5.2 million	$23,269	3.5	$439
5-State Mean	—	$24,095	4.4	$404
U.S.	—	$24,231	5.5	$377

Table 1-1
Demographic and Economic Characteristics
of Five Midwestern States

Source: *Statistical Abstract of the United States: 1997*, tables 26, 626, and 706; *1996 Green Book: Overview of Entitlement Programs*, http://www.aspe.os.dhhs.gov.

The story of welfare reform in the Midwest is also significant because these states have strong elements of what Elazar (1984) calls moralistic political cultures and are not known for their harsh social policies or heartless disregard for the poor. Indeed, the five states we will examine awarded average AFDC monthly payments per family in 1995 substantially higher than those of the nation, despite per capita incomes very close to the national average (see Table 1-1). Yet these states quickly embraced the notion of requiring welfare recipients to take personal responsibility and put work first, often imposing relatively harsh sanctions requiring mothers of very young children to work soon after birth. How and why these states came to embrace these policies in a relatively short period of time is both interesting and noteworthy.

The Politics of Enactment

The politics of welfare reform in the five Midwestern states shared more similarities than differences, with reform efforts encountering few disagreements and raised voices. Democrats and Republicans across the five states largely agreed that past policies were not working, and that a new approach requiring a person to find and keep a job was admirable. In Wisconsin, members of a welfare coalition agreed early on that they would not try to defeat the overall initiative but rather would attempt to change the program on its margins. In Michigan and Minnesota, new state legislation built on successful existing programs, thus alleviating some possible concern about the effects on recipients.

The task at hand is not to explain the variation among the five Midwestern states, or even to show how these states differ from the other 45. Rather, we will focus on the elements contributing to successful implementation common across the five states: the strong local economies, the political entrepreneurship of the Republican governors, and a record of earlier pilot programs and requests for waivers from federal guidelines that initiated a process of incremental reform.

The Midwest Economy

In the mid-1990s, the Midwest economy was booming. While the U.S. unemployment rate hovered at 5.4 percent in 1996, for example, the rate in these five states averaged 4.4 percent (see Table 1-1). Wisconsin — one of the leaders in welfare reform — boasted a 3.5 percent unemployment rate.

Throughout the Midwest, employers were begging for workers. The director of Michigan's Department of Social Services, Gerald Miller, told audiences that requests for employees helped drive his support for work-focused welfare reform. Similarly, in Wisconsin and Minnesota, the strength of the state economy and the ready availability of jobs were important in assuaging Democrats and liberal advocates that a fundamental change in approach might make sense.

The strong economy also likely played an important role in ensuring political and public acceptance of work first as fundamental to welfare reform. Early welfare reform efforts, undertaken in part to cut welfare programs and budgets in response to recession-induced fiscal problems, had prompted very different political reactions. Norris and Thompson (1995) described the welfare reform politics of the early 1990s in six states (including Michigan, Ohio, and Wisconsin) as having a high political profile, provoking considerable disagreement between the governor and the legislature, and being "highly conflictual." Yet later welfare reform measures engendered very little conflict between governor and legislature and no noticeable public outcry. Even the strongest welfare advocates had to agree that jobs could be had by welfare clients.

Table 1-2 TANF Recipients, Allocations and Caseload Reductions in the Midwest				
	Number of TANF Recipients September 1998	Basic TANF Allocation	Percentage Drop in Caseload 1993-98	Percentage Drop in Caseload 1996-98
Kansas	63,783	$102 million	-63%	-49%
Michigan	502,354	$775 million	-59%	-44%
Minnesota	169,744	$268 million	-28%	-19%
Ohio	549,312	$728 million	-56%	-42%
Wisconsin	148,888	$318 million	-86%	-77%
5-State Mean			-58%	-46%
U.S.	—	—	-46%	-38%

Source: U.S. Department of Health and Human Services Administration for Children and Families, http://www.acf.dhhs.gov/news/stats/caseload.htm, and Lazere 1999, p. 15.

The healthy economy provided not only an impetus for change but also the resources to fund a new approach. The economy has been linked to the recent dramatic drops in welfare caseload in many states, including those in the Midwest (Blank 1997, Gais 1997). Four of these five Midwestern states saw caseloads drop at a greater rate than that of the national average, even before federal reform (see Table 1-2). The Council of Economic Advisors (1997) estimated that 44 percent of this decline resulted from the improving economy. The federal reform also helped greatly by basing TANF block grant allocations on federal grants paid from 1992 to 1995, when welfare caseloads and spending reached historic highs.

The recent dramatic reductions in caseloads have allowed states to use relatively large amounts of funds to serve fewer people. The Government Accounting Office (GAO) has concluded that the "combination of the decline in caseload levels, the higher federal grant levels and the maintenance of effort requirement for the states' contribution to the programs means that most states have more budgetary resources available for their low-income family assistance programs since enactment of welfare reform than under prior law" (Government Accounting Office 1998a, p. 10). The GAO found that 45 states received more in federal resources from TANF than they received in the year prior to reform.

Indeed, the five Midwestern states posted a mean difference of 25 percent between the TANF block grant and what they would have received before reform; the national mean difference was only 13 percent. In Wisconsin, the expenses in the first year of TANF ran much less than expected, according to Thomas Kaplan. In a chapter in this volume, Kaplan reports that Wisconsin saved some $100 million under the first year of reform, with $36 million of that targeted to reinvest in the communities.

Gubernatorial Leadership

All five governors in office when their states adopted welfare reform were Republican. In four of the five states, the same Republican governor led the state throughout the 1991-1998 time period (see Table 1-3).

Table 1-3 Midwest Gubernatorial Leadership 1991-98		
	1991-94	*1995-98*
Kansas	Joan Finney (D)	Bill Graves (R)
Michigan	John Engler (R)	John Engler (R)
Minnesota	Arne Carlson (R)	Arne Carlson (R)
Ohio	George Voinovich (R)	George Voinovich (R)
Wisconsin	Tommy Thompson (R)	Tommy Thompson (R)
SOURCE: Council of State Governments, *The Book of the States*, various editions.		

6

In four of the five states, Republican governors were strong political leaders, if not policy entrepreneurs (Bardach 1972, Weissert 1991, Oliver and Paul-Shaheen 1997). Governors Engler and Thompson were highly visible leaders who relied on the mass media to pursue their goals. Both identified welfare reform as a top priority, and both yoked their political success to it. Governor Engler, especially, links his political capital to the success of welfare reform. He continues to issue monthly press releases on his state's program, especially a demonstration project entitled Project Zero, which aims to reduce the number of unemployed recipients in targeted counties to zero. Tommy Thompson made welfare reform a major issue in his campaign for governor in 1986, promising to reduce AFDC benefits and stop what he claimed was welfare-induced migration to the state. Like Engler, Thompson is not given to modesty. Thomas Kaplan quotes from a 1998 Thompson press release that boasts, "Ours was the first welfare-to-work program in the nation, and it remains a model for other states to follow."

Ironically, it was Democrats in Wisconsin who stepped up that state's advance in welfare reform by arguing that the governor's 1993 "Work Not Welfare" proposal merely tinkered with the system, when what it really needed was replacement. Wisconsin Democrats demanded that AFDC must be replaced by a wholly new system before December 31, 1998, that included childcare, health care, and public-sector jobs for people who could work but were unable to find employment. The governor, using his extensive item veto power, retained the language eliminating AFDC yet deleted all the programmatic directives. As Kaplan puts it, the "governor had thus crafted a requirement that a cabinet agency under his direct control propose an indeterminate replacement for a welfare system now mandated to end."

Governors also played key roles in Ohio and Minnesota. Governor Voinovich of Ohio was initially unsuccessful in his attempts to end general assistance and eliminate barriers to employment of welfare recipients. But with the help of a strong human services director, the governor could claim success in 1995 when the legislature set time limits on cash assistance, required recipients to either work or participate in education to retain welfare benefits, and provided one-time payments for recipients' special needs that might pose barriers to employability. Minnesota's governor set up a bipartisan task force composed of legislators and state welfare officials to develop recommendations following the passage of PRWORA. Four months later, legislation was enacted

In Kansas, the governor's role was much more muted and did not play out in press releases and media attention. Nonetheless he was an important force in crafting what Jocelyn Johnston and Kara Lindaman in this volume dub "a reform environment that precluded vigorous legislative intervention." In so doing, the governor maintained the moderate tenor of welfare policy changes despite punitive approaches favored by more conservative members of his party.

Agenda setting has long been one of the primary roles of governors in public policy formation (Schneider 1989, Rosenthal 1990, Herzik 1991, Beyle 1999). Each of these governors used his powers to put welfare reform on his state's policy agenda. But the governors did more than set the agenda: they outlined their vision for welfare reform and used their political resources to translate their vision into policy. For example, when Michigan's Project Zero sites do not raise the number of clients with earned income to the goal, the directors receive a call from the governor's office, and must submit a report detailing the reasons for the shortfall. Several governors have also continued to pursue changes in welfare after the initial reform legislation.

Governors Thompson and Engler clearly utilized their informal powers to garner press attention and eventually public acclaim for their efforts. Both were active in Washington debates and were cognizant of their roles as leaders in federal and state welfare reform efforts. Thomas Kaplan notes that Governor Thompson's first waiver request in July 1993 was widely viewed as the governor's attempt to beat President Bill Clinton to a time-limited welfare system. Carol Weissert describes the role that Governor Engler's national political aspirations were felt to play in the swift passage of Michigan welfare reform legislation in December 1995.[2]

In Ohio, Kansas, Michigan, and Wisconsin, the head of the welfare agency was also key to the success of welfare reform. In a chapter in this book, Charles Adams and Miriam Wilson describe how Ohio's Governor Voinovich was roundly criticized for his early attempts at devising welfare reform largely without consulting legislative and interest group leaders. A welfare director hired in 1993 worked to develop strong relationships with these leaders, especially between the department and the legislative committees responsible for welfare. In Kansas, the welfare department and its director were the primary force for policy change. In Michigan, the social services director was a major player in the design and initial implementation of the state welfare policy, and also worked with Washington officials on federal legislation. In Wisconsin, the head of the state welfare division was a key figure in the executive branch committee that designed the state's welfare reform legislation.

The legislative role in the Midwest was clearly reactive to governors' proposals. This legislative responsiveness may have stemmed from the recognition by politicians of both parties of the need for change in the delivery of welfare services. Legislators seemed reluctant to argue for the status quo, and put few other policy plans on the table to compete with the work-first notions. Ohio's plan in 1997 passed unanimously in both houses. Minnesota's legislature adopted a plan based on the governor's framework with relatively few objections early in the legislative session. Interestingly, party control is not the explanation for this quiescence. In only one state — Kansas — did Republicans control both houses throughout the period of welfare reform. Governor Thompson faced a Democratic House with his early reforms, and Governor Carlson faced Democratic legislatures throughout the early and mid-1990s (see Table 1-4).

Table 1-4 Party Control in Midwest Legislatures				
	1991-92 Senate House	*1993-94 Senate House*	*1995-96 Senate House*	*1997-98 Senate House*
Kansas	R R	R R	R R	R R
Michigan	R D	R Tie	R R	R D
Minnesota	D D	D D	D D	D D
Ohio	R D	R D	R R	R R
Wisconsin	R D	R D	R R	D R
SOURCE: *The Book of the States,* various editions.				

Other actors proved important in the story of welfare reform. Several governors set up blue ribbon commissions or task forces, and foundations and think tanks were very much involved in formulating policy in Wisconsin. However, these efforts were secondary to those of both elected and appointed leaders of the executive branch.

Evolution, Not Revolution

In these five states, the welfare reform packages of the mid-1990s saw their genesis in initiatives, waivers, and proposals of earlier years (see Table 1-5). The five states averaged six prereform waivers, compared with a national average of only four. For Michigan, Wisconsin, Ohio, and Kansas, the predecessor programs established from federal waivers, or the federal Job Opportunities and Basic Skills Training (JOBS) program, were important building blocks for implementation of the TANF program. Minnesota's welfare reform plan, for example, built on two earlier initiatives — a pilot welfare program, entitled the Minnesota Family Investment Program (MFIP), and a jobs program, Success Through Reaching Individual Development and Employment (STRIDE). State leaders also incorporated an innovative health program called MinnesotaCare into their welfare reform initiative. Thus, while some reform packages represented large-scale changes, they stemmed from pilot programs that not only tested the ideas but also cushioned political opposition. Thomas Kaplan described the changes in Wisconsin, for example, as emerging "only gradually and haltingly from a decade of experimentation."

Table 1-5 Pre-Reform Waiver Provision		
	Number of Pre-Reform Waiver Provisions Adopted[1]	*Date of State Welfare Reform Legislation*
Kansas	5	NA
Michigan	7	December 1995
Minnesota	5	April 1997
Ohio	7	July 1997
Wisconsin	6	April 1996
5-State Mean	6	
U.S. Mean	4.0	

SOURCE: General Accounting Office. *Welfare Reform: States Are Restructuring Programs to Reduce Welfare Dependence*, 1998.

1   The GAO (1998) documented nine possible waiver provisions, including: lowered age of youngest child exemption to under one year, established full-family sanction for noncooperation with work requirements, increased asset limits over $1,000 and/or vehicle allowances over $1,500, changed earned income disregard policies, imposed time limits on the receipt of benefits for entire family, liberalized 100-hour or labor force attachment rules for two-parent families, established full-family sanction for noncooperation with child support enforcement requirements, allowed or required noncustodial parents to participate in JOBS, imposed teen living and/or teen school attendance requirements.

Thus, overall, the politics of welfare reform were shaped in these states by a strong economy, dominant Republican governors, and prior policy initiatives.

Putting New Policies into Action

One of the most striking commonalities across the five states is the emphasis on work first strategies. Although PRWORA sent a clear signal to states that welfare reform should emphasize work first, these five Midwestern states had already adopted this goal.

Indeed, each of the five Midwestern states established programs that emphasized job search and de-emphasized education and training for that job. Wisconsin's system places recipients on one of four "rungs" of self-sufficiency. Recipients on the transition and community service rungs are expected to work their way up to unsubsidized employment, the top rung. In Michigan, and elsewhere in the Midwest, training and education assistance is very limited.[3] Kansas provides limited job training only during the first 60 days of assistance to those with poor or low skills, although it has recently intensified its employment preparation services for those with substantial barriers to employment.

Funding pilot programs is a popular mechanism for the Midwestern states. Michigan's Project Zero is an example of such a pilot, which started in 6 counties in the first year and grew to 35 in the third year of funding. Project Zero provides additional resources to welfare offices to reduce the number of recipients not working to zero. Ohio has a TANF Early Start pilot in five counties that identifies at-risk infants. These programs enhance the receptivity of the offices or counties (as well as legislators) to reform, since they demonstrate what problems can arise and how resources might best be used.

Contrasts in Implementation

Yet despite their similarities in goals and politics, the Midwest states have varied greatly in their implementation of welfare reform, especially in how they have devolved responsibility to local governments and nonprofit agencies and demanded accountability.

11

The states also differ in their imposition of time limits, exemptions for new mothers, earnings disregards, transitional Medicaid and childcare benefits, maximum benefit levels and benefits for additional children, and sanctions for noncompliance. Table 1-6 provides an overview of these substantive components of the states' welfare programs.

Given their unique reform packages, the states are hard to classify as liberal or conservative, tough or lenient. For example, Michigan has refused to establish a time limit for welfare recipients, and has proposed supporting those who exceed the five-year federal time limit with state dollars. Yet Michigan also expects mothers to work when their child is three months old and provides relatively modest benefits. It also recently became the first state to subject all TANF applicants to drug testing (initially in five pilot counties). Wisconsin does not increase family benefits when more children are born but supports recipients who perform community service relatively generously.

All the states do impose moderately tough sanctions. Wisconsin's case is among the most interesting. Sanctions were relatively rare in the early months of implementation of the W-2 welfare reform program, according to Thomas Kaplan. But in December 1997 the state's chief administrator of W-2 wrote to the implementing agencies urging greater use of sanctions where appropriate. Shortly thereafter between 26 and 29 percent of all participants in the two lower rungs were sanctioned. Any time a participant misses hours of assignment in W-2 transition or community service without good cause, her monthly grant is reduced by $5.15 an hour. Ohio maintains a three-tiered sanction policy that withholds 100 percent of participants' assistance grants from one to six months, as well as the adult portion of their food stamp benefits. Kansas and Michigan withhold the entire grant allotment for families of participants who fail to meet work standards.

The combination of harsh and more supportive policies within each state program makes them difficult to rank. For example, in a ranking by Tufts University's Center on Hunger and Poverty (1998), only Minnesota appeared in the top 15 states in the fairness of its program (ranking 12th). Michigan was ranked 28th, Wisconsin 30th, Ohio 38th, and Kansas 49th of 51 jurisdictions (including the District of Columbia).[4] The study authors themselves note the complexity of state policies, providing Michigan as an example of a state

Learning From Midwestern Leaders

Table 1-6 Characteristics of TANF Programs Across Five Midwestern States

	Kansas	Michigan	Minnesota	Ohio	Wisconsin[2]
Time Limit	60 months	None	60 months	36 months[1]	60 months[2]
Age of Youngest-Child Exemption for Work	Under age 1	Under age 12 weeks[3]	Under age 1	Under age 1	Under age 12 weeks
Earnings Disregard	$90 plus 40% is disregarded	$200 plus 20% is disregarded	36% of gross earnings	$250 plus 50% is disregarded[4]	Disregarded until family reaches 115% of poverty level
Transitional Medicaid	12 months	12 months	12 months	12 months	12 months
Transitional Childcare	All families up to 185% of the federal poverty level, regardless of program status[5]	24 months[6]	12 months	12 months	All families up to 200% of the federal poverty level, regardless of program status.
Maximum Benefit Level For Family of Three	$429	$459 (Detroit)	$532	$362	$673 for family in community service; $628 for family in transition
Family Cap	No	No	No	No	Yes
Sanction for Noncompliance with individual responsibility plan	Termination; sanctions are suspended as soon as the client complies with program requirements	Reduction, removal of individual or termination	Reduction, removal of individual	Condition of eligibility	Loss of $5.15 for every hour out of compliance (termination allowed under the law)

Source: U.S. Department of Health and Human Services, *Temporary Assistance for Needy Families Program: First Annual Report to Congress*, August 1998.

1 Recipients can receive cash benefit for up to three years. Once limit is reached, participants cannot collect benefits for at least two years. After that, they can apply for another two years if they need additional assistance and can show good cause why they cannot find work.
2 Only 24 months in any one tier of the four tiers of the W-2 program.
3 In DHHS's First Annual Report to Congress, Michigan is listed as not providing automatic exemptions. However, the state in its TANF report indicated that deferred persons included the mother of a child under the age of 3 months.
4 An 18-month time limit was eliminated as of July 1, 1999.
5 Two months after case closing, families may be subject to a sliding scale fee based on income.
6 After 12 months, there is a sliding scale and recipients receive day care benefits according to their level of income.

that relies on both negative sanctions and positive incentives to move people off welfare. Another problem with this and other rankings is the difficulty of developing measures that reflect how the program is actually implemented. For example, while both Michigan and Wisconsin have significantly increased their spending for childcare and made the service available to those with incomes well over poverty on a sliding scale, Wisconsin's program has been undersubscribed and Michigan's has not. Minnesota's childcare program has a waiting list of over 7,000; Michigan is able to accept participants without waiting. A final problem is the changing nature of programs, which makes rankings based on one point in time misleading.

The chapters in this book explore the policies of the five Midwestern states more fully to provide advanced understanding that such large-scale rankings and studies cannot capture.

Devolution and Accountability

Rather than the command-and-control approach of AFDC, which prescribed welfare policy and regulated state administrative activities, TANF allows states considerable discretion to either retain control over welfare programs or devolve funds and responsibilities to counties, workforce development boards, or nonprofit agencies, including religious groups. In fact, states can choose not to provide cash assistance at all (Schram and Weissert 1997). Yet in return for this administrative freedom, states must report the results of their programs to the federal government.

State Administrative Change

The Midwestern states studied here have clearly taken advantage of the opportunity in PRWORA to revamp their administrative structure implementing welfare — and sometimes other programs. The states moved quickly and decisively, typically assigning responsibilities to state agencies dealing with welfare and labor or workforce issues.

Each of the five states made major changes in state administration and/or staff assignments and duties. Minnesota, Michigan, and Wisconsin set up new or newly named departments that emphasized the work-first approach. Wisconsin, for example, switched all public assistance functions (except Medicaid) to the Department of Industry, Labor and Human Relations, then changed the agency's name to the Department of Workforce Development. Michigan too changed the agency's name to reflect the new emphasis — from the Department of Social Services to the Family Independence Agency. Ohio is considering a consolidation of its employment and welfare agencies. Table 1-7 provides an overview of the organization of the states' welfare programs.

Table 1-7 Types of State Agencies With Primary Responsibility Over Employment, Cash Assistance, and Child Care Functions			
State	*Employment and Training*	*Cash Assistance*	*Child Care*
1. Employment bureaucracy shares responsibilities for job services with social service agency			
Kansas	Department of Human Resources Social and Rehabilitation Services	Social and Rehabilitation Services	Social and Rehabilitation Services
Ohio	Department of Human Services[1] Department of Development Bureau of Employment Services	Department of Human Services	
2. Employment agencies have dominant responsibility for employment and training			
Michigan	Department of Career Development	Family Independence Agency	
Minnesota	Department of Economic Security	Department of Human Services	Department of Children, Families and Learning
Wisconsin	Department of Workforce Development		

1 State law calls for the Ohio Department of Human Services and the Ohio Bureau of Employment Services to be combined into the Ohio Department of Job and Family Services by July 1, 2000.

In Wisconsin, income maintenance workers became financial and employment planners; in Michigan, eligibility workers became family independence specialists; Kansas combined former income maintenance and employment preparation positions into new caseworker positions. Ohio added a new position called account managers, borrowing a term from the private sector.

In states such as Michigan, Kansas, and Ohio, where two separate state agencies formerly coordinated employment and eligibility functions, combining state agencies has sometimes proved difficult. An issue for a number of Midwestern states has been changing the cultures of the agencies responsible for the new programs — from one where the key issue for staff is determining eligibility to one where the focus is on helping clients help themselves, from issuing checks to finding jobs. In Michigan, for example, the welfare agency and the jobs agency had little experience in working together. A reticence or unwillingness among state agencies to share welfare and jobs information has also been a problem in Ohio.

More successful in Kansas has been the state human services agency's effort to work with the rehabilitation services and corrections agency, the University of Kansas, and other organizations to refine tools for diagnosing learning disabilities that will be used to assess clients' initial employability.

In short, the five Midwestern states made major substantive changes in the organization of agencies responsible for implementing welfare reform. These changes have required some cultural changes in the agencies' staff, as welfare workers are encouraged to help clients become more independent, rather than to meet their needs through making aid and other assistance available to them.

To Centralize or Decentralize Authority

The five states differ substantially in the way they divide responsibility for administering TANF among state and local entities. Michigan and Kansas are state-supervised and administered systems; Minnesota, Ohio, and Wisconsin are state-supervised and locally administered. However, these classifications understate differences among the systems. For example, Michigan's local welfare offices are staffed with state employees who traditionally have had little interaction with local government. However, on the employment side of Michigan's welfare reform initiative, funds flow to workforce development boards that have much closer relationships with local employers and county officials.

In Ohio, the most decentralized program among the five, each county operates independently but with a common mission and set of activities. The county boards sign partnership agreements with the state department of health specifying expectations of county performance and state contributions. Under the agreement, the counties receive block grants that represent pooled state funds for human service programs. The counties also work closely with each other, developing networks and sharing informal advice without assistance from the state. In Wisconsin, decentralized services are sometimes provided by counties and sometimes by private agencies.

To improve coordination between state and counties and alleviate possible conflicts, several states have important regional components to their delivery of services. In Ohio, account managers in each of 12 regions serve as liaison between the counties and the state. These managers assess county performance and provide feedback to both county and state. They also connect the county with state-level technical training and support. As part of its recent reform, Kansas has given regional offices greater responsibility for administering welfare. Wisconsin's W-2 program identified geographic areas for local administration and, where the existing agency did not win a right of first selection, allowed any agency — public or private, profit or not-for-profit — to bid to provide services.

In Minnesota, some state-local difficulties have arisen over the uneven distribution of TANF education and training funds to counties. As Thomas Luce notes in a chapter in this volume, one county's average funding per case was 72 percent of the state average, while another's was some 246 percent of the state average — a difference of over $1,400 per case.

Ohio, Kansas, and Michigan have also encouraged nonprofit and private agencies to become involved in delivering TANF services. Ohio has launched pilot state projects with local neighborhood and faith-based community organizations. When the Ohio legislature appropriated $5 million for involving community-based organizations in welfare reform, over 200 organizations applied for funding.

Such moves have raised questions about accountability. Ohio chose a private-industry model of accountability in which county "franchisees" operate independently but must meet performance objectives. In Michigan, the Department of Career Development has limited oversight over the workforce development boards responsible for training and job assistance; nearly all the TANF dollars directed to work-related issues flow to the local boards. In neither of these cases is anyone monitoring the types of jobs recipients are finding nor assessing what type of assistance they require along the way.

Decentralization is part and parcel of what Nathan and Gais (1999) call "second-order devolution" where the states are providing greater responsibilities to local governments which in turn often hand over program responsibilities to non-profit and for-profit organizations under contracts. This is certainly the case in the five Midwestern states examined here. Even strong-state supervised systems like that in Michigan have devolved a great deal of discretion to regional workforce development boards which utilize very different approaches to providing job assistance to clients. Ohio's devolution has been the most dramatic, with counties operating the welfare program independently following broad state guidelines.

Federal Monitoring

The new federal law shifted the focus from management reporting to performance-based reporting. If states do not meet statutory requirements specifying the percentages of caseloads participating in work or work-related activities, they will incur financial penalties.[5] Federal "bonuses" go to the five states that have most success in lowering their teenage pregnancy rates, and to the ten states that achieve the most success in helping welfare recipients find jobs and earn income. The U.S. Department of Health and Human Services (DHHS) uses the states' reporting to rank states annually on the percentage of participants they place in long-term private-sector jobs, the number of children living in poverty, and the reductions in percentage of out-of-wedlock births (GAO 1998b). States must submit detailed quarterly data reports to DHHS, collecting information they had often not previously collected on clients' work participation, hours worked, the types of work and the services they receive, and the reasons people leave welfare. States are also required to report on the activities they engage in with their "maintenance-of-effort funds" — the state dollars spent on welfare. Federal law requires states to maintain effort equal to 75 percent to 80 percent of their own spending in 1994.

The success of states' response will rely in large part on the quality of their management information systems. However, many states are struggling to change systems geared for management reporting to those geared to reflect performance, especially in tracking participants' success in getting and keeping jobs. Nathan and Gais (1998) have contended that "if there is any major weakness in the implementation of the new welfare, data systems are it."

The problem stems partly from the very flexibility the federal welfare law now allows. In Michigan, for example, the Family Independence Agency, responsible for cash assistance, and the Michigan Department of Career Development, responsible for employment and training, have different information systems. Local officers must manually re-enter data from one system into another. What's more, this information is often considered proprietary. There is so little interaction among agencies handling this information that in one state key welfare agency computing staff did not even know their counterparts in the jobs agency. A further concern is making certain that such data are accessible to counties for their own use — an important issue in states choosing to decentralize considerable responsibility to local governments. Ohio, for example, has struggled with how to set up an integrated system that will collect the data necessary for federal reporting but also provide information useful to the counties. To solve such problems, the state has decided to devote considerable funds from its welfare-related surplus to create an integrated management information system. In Kansas, local area offices complain that the reports generated by the state are virtually useless. Decentralization clearly complicates reporting and the accountability that flows from it. The more decentralized the services, the harder the task of describing, monitoring and evaluating the results. This is one of the major paradoxes of welfare reform in the Midwest and elsewhere. A skeptical Congress considering reauthorization of PRWORA in 2002 may well question the benefit of decentralization if it comes at the cost of limited accountability.

Evaluation. Another important aspect of monitoring is evaluation — studies designed to provide more policy-relevant information than the performance-based approach. These studies can answer questions such as: Is the state saving money under welfare reform? What happens to families sanctioned under the new policies? Are former clients succeeding in developing long-term careers?

Support for evaluation varies widely across the states. Ohio and Wisconsin are coordinating internal and external evaluation and research efforts, which in the case of Wisconsin are extensive. For example, Wisconsin's Governor Thompson created the Management and Evaluation Project, which both stimulates evaluation projects and reviews proposals made by others. It also formally sponsors projects that may obtain data from the state more easily than outside studies. In Ohio, a number of outside evaluations are examining caseload dynamics and closed cases evaluating the state program more broadly. In contrast, Michigan has very limited evaluation efforts under way. Even its widely self-touted Project Zero is not being evaluated systematically to assess its effectiveness.

Conclusion

These five Midwestern states adopted and implemented welfare reform without acrimony and with considerable enthusiasm. While there were major differences among the states, particularly in the implementation of the reforms, there were also many similarities.

Governors played primary direct and indirect roles in shaping welfare reform. The changes that occurred after passage of the 1996 federal law built on earlier efforts the states had undertaken and have been integrated into health, education, and child-protection programs already under way. The region's strong economy has been a major contributor to the implementation efforts, allowing states to pursue work-first strategies without political opposition. The lower welfare rolls and stable federal funding have provided the states with financial windfalls that have been used for innovative or expanded programs that might not otherwise be possible.

Each of the five Midwestern states examined in this volume has made substantive changes in providing welfare and job-related services. They have reorganized state departments and devolved some authority to counties, nonprofits, and private agencies. They continue to make changes in the programs and to deal with problems of coordination and equity.

The Midwestern states have differed in their willingness to share implementation responsibility with counties and nonprofits. Ohio — at one extreme — is highly decentralized to the point that it is difficult to generalize across the counties. Michigan and Kansas, in contrast, have not relinquished power to counties but have decentralized some functions to regional offices (Kansas) and to workforce development boards (Michigan).

While it is difficult to say that the experiences and lessons of these states reflect those of other states, it is safe to say that they are being repeated in a number of other regions, and that insights from the midwestern experiences can provide useful guidance to state officials, researchers, and advocates evaluating the progress of one of the most significant laws of the 1990s.

References

Bardach, Eugene. 1972. *The Skill Factor in Politics*. Berkeley: University of California Press.

Beyle, Thad. 1999. The Governors in *Politics in the American States: A Comparative Analysis*, 7th ed., Virginia Gray, Russell Hanson, and Herbert Jacob, eds. Washington, DC: Congressional Quarterly Press.

Blank, Rebecca. 1997. What Causes Public Assistance Caseloads to Grow. Evanston, IL: Northwestern University

Center on Hunger and Poverty. 1998. *Are States Improving the Lives of Poor Families? A Scale Measure of State Welfare Policies*. Medford, MA: Tufts University.

Council of Economic Advisers. 1997. *Explaining the Decline in Welfare Receipt 1993-1996*, Washington, DC: CEA.

Council of State Governments. *Book of the States 1992-93, 1994-95, 1996-98.* Lexington, KY: CSG.

Elazar, Daniel. 1984. *American Federalism: A View from the States*, 3rd ed. New York: W.W. Norton.

Francis, Richard. 1999. Predictions, Patterns, and Policymaking: A Regional Study of Devolution. *Publius: The Journal of Federalism* 28, 3: 143-160.

Gais, Thomas J. 1997. The Relationship of the Decline in Welfare Cases to the New Welfare Law: How Will We Know if It Is Working? *Rockefeller Report.* Albany, NY: The Nelson Rockefeller Institute of Government.

General Accounting Office. 1998a. *Welfare Reform: Early Fiscal Effects of the TANF Block Grant*, August. Washington DC: GAO.

General Accounting Office. 1998b. *Welfare Reform: States Are Restructuring Programs to Reduce Welfare Dependence.* June. Washington, DC: GAO.

Herzik, Eric B. 1991. Policy Agendas and Gubernatorial Leadership. In *Gubernatorial Leadership and State Policy*, Eric B. Herzik and Brent W. Brown, eds. New York: Greenwood Press, 25-37.

Lazere, Ed. 1999. *Unspent TANF Funds at the End of the Federal Fiscal Year 1998.* Washington, DC: Center on Budget and Policy Priorities.

Nathan, Richard P. and Thomas L. Gais. 1998. *Implementation of the Personal Responsibility Act of 1996.* Albany, NY: The Nelson Rockefeller Institute of Government.

Nathan, Richard P. and Thomas L. Gais. 1999. Early Findings about the Newest New Federalism for Welfare. *Publius: The Journal of Federalism* 28,3:95-103.

Norris, Donald F. and Lyke Thompson. 1995. Findings and Lessons from the Politics of Welfare Reform. In *The Politics of Welfare Reform*, Donald F. Norris and Lyke Thompson, eds. Thousand Oaks, CA: Sage Publications.

Oliver, Thomas R. and Pamela Paul-Shaheen. 1997. Translating Ideas into Actions: Entrepreneurial Leadership in State Health Care Reforms. *Journal of Health Politics, Policy and Law* 22,3: 721-788.

Rosenthal, Alan. 1990. *Governors and Legislatures: Contending Powers.* Washington, DC: Congressional Quarterly Press.

Schneider, Saundra K. 1989. Governors and Health Care Policy in the American States. *Policy Studies Journal* 17,4: 909-926.

Schram, Sanford F. and Carol S. Weissert. 1997. The State of American Federalism 1996-1997. *Publius: The Journal of Federalism* 27,2: 1-31.

U.S. Bureau of the Census. 1997. *Statistical Abstract of the United States,* Washington, DC: Government Printing Office.

U.S. House of Representative, Committee on Ways and Means. *1996 Green Book: Overview of Entitlement Programs.* World Wide Web: Internet Citation: http://www.aspe.os.dhhs.gov.

U.S. Department of Health and Human Services. 1998. *Temporary Assistance for Needy Families Program: First Annual Report to Congress,* Washington, DC: Government Printing Office.

Weaver, R. Kent. 1996. Deficits and Devolution in the 104th Congress. *Publius: The Journal of Federalism* 26, 3: 45-85.

Weissert, Carol S. 1991. Policy Entrepreneurs, Policy Opportunists, and Legislative Effectiveness. *American Politics Quarterly* 19,2: 262-274.

Weissert, Carol S. and Sanford F. Schram. 1996. The State of American Federalism, 1995-1996. *Publius: The Journal of Federalism* 26,3: 1-26.

Endnotes

1   Research on welfare reform has been conducted by the Assessing the New Federalism project at the Urban Institute, the Rockefeller Institute of Government, the General Accounting Office, the Center on Hunger and Poverty at Tufts University, the National Governors' Association, the National Conference of State Legislatures, the Welfare Information Network and the American Public Welfare Association, and dozens of individual academics and policy analysts.

2   Interestingly, in some states the gubernatorial role has been described as much less significant. For example, in examining the New England states Francis (1999) found that administrative officials, not politicians, were leading welfare reform. There are several possible reasons for the startling different roles of governors in the Midwest and New England. First, the New England governors have fewer institutional powers than those of the Midwestern governors and other governors across the country. The six New England governors have a mean score of 3.1 in their institutional powers (out of a possible 5). The five Midwestern governors have a mean score of 3.7; the mean from governors across the country was 3.4 (Beyle 1999). Beyle also reports a measure of the personal powers of governors in 1998. Since the list of governors in 1998 is not identical to the governors in 1996, the scale is not as meaningful, but the same trends appear. The Midwestern governors score 4.2; the New England governors' mean is 3.6; the national mean is 3.8. It is important to note that state administrators are part of the executive branch and funded by the state legislature, and thus are usually well aware of gubernatorial and legislative policy preferences. In most states, the governors play an important role in the policy direction and certainly the policy priorities of the state bureaucracy.

3   In Fall 1999, Michigan implemented a new program providing more liberal training and education policies.

4   The Tufts scale evaluated benefit levels and eligibility, time limits, work requirements and sanctions, assistance obtaining work, income and asset development, childcare assistance, and policies toward legal immigrants' families.

5   States must have 25 percent of recipients from one-parent families working at least 20 hours a week by the end of 1997. These requirements rise to 50 percent working at least 30 hours a week by year 2002. Goals were also set for two-parent families. Failure to meet these rates can reduce a state's block grant by 5 percent in the first year eventually going to 21 percent.

Chapter 2

WELFARE REFORM MEETS THE DEVOLUTION REVOLUTION IN OHIO

Charles F. Adams and Miriam S. Wilson

The most recent wave of welfare reform in Ohio began in 1995 with legislation that emphasized client self-sufficiency, time limits, and requirements for education and workforce participation. This effort continued with 1997 legislation, passed in response to the federal TANF, that broadened the state's focus to include greater county control over the design and implementation of local welfare systems. Ohio has also emphasized the importance of community involvement in welfare reform, not only as advisory groups but also as direct service providers.

In pursuing its brand of welfare reform, the state sought guidance not so much from what other states were doing but from the private sector — specifically, the business franchise model exemplified by the Wendy's Corporation. Early in the reform process, senior staff from the Ohio Department of Human Services (ODHS) met with senior executives of Wendy's to better understand the franchise model and its possible adaptation in restructuring Ohio's welfare system. Under the plan that resulted from this model, the commissioners in each of Ohio's 88 counties serve as franchisees, partnership agreements between ODHS and each county provide the legal link establishing this relationship, and the new ODHS account managers serve as their counterparts in corporate head-quarters in monitoring performance.

That Ohio should adopt such a corporate model is not surprising given that the state is led by a Republican governor and has a Republican majority in both houses of the legislature. The governor recruited a senior administrator from the Reagan-Bush Department of Health and Human Services to head up ODHS, and filled other top administrative positions in ODHS with persons recruited from county-run human service agencies. For Ohio, welfare reform has meant thinking more like a business, with a primary emphasis on the role of counties as franchisees whose performance would ultimately determine the success or failure of the state's reform efforts.

Ohio also has a long tradition of strong county government. Counties take the funding and organizational lead in a wide range of human services, including child support, children services, alcohol and drug abuse, mental retardation, and aging services. Welfare reform under TANF has further strengthened county government in Ohio, with devolution of decision making authority from state to county government in the design and implementation of welfare-related support services. Instead of a human services structure largely designed and supervised at the state level, Ohio now has 88 separate welfare programs.

Over 24 months have now passed since the state began to implement this model, so it is appropriate to ask, "Where's the beef?" The answer turns importantly on a number of indicators of success: Whether the program has succeeded in moving people from welfare to work, in keeping people off welfare to begin with, and in ensuring that those who leave welfare stay off. It's success also hinges on whether state administrators have given local managers the freedom to act creatively in designing local service delivery systems, and on whether these local managers have capitalized on such opportunities.

While still very much a work in progress, Ohio has had at least partial success in reforming its welfare system along these lines. Caseloads have fallen, and some part of that reduction is presumably due to reform efforts, although the extent to which those leaving the system are successfully transitioning to regular employment and self-sufficiency is unknown. The state has recently awarded a contract for a systematic study of welfare clients whose cases have closed. For those on the welfare rolls, outcomes regarding work participation are mixed.[1]

Institutionally, 79 partnership agreements between ODHS and county departments of human services were signed as of August 1999, granting these counties access to monies based on performance incentives and giving them much wider discretion in organizing and packaging TANF-related support services. The newly created account manager positions within ODHS have been posted and filled. And, most significantly, all 88 Ohio counties now have Prevention, Retention, and Contingency (PRC) programs, an innovative effort to marshal an array of services designed to keep people from needing regular welfare assistance, and to limit reentry into the welfare system by former recipients. Counties have considerable discretion in deciding how much of their TANF funding to allocate to PRC programs, and state officials have expressed concern that counties are being too conservative, with only about $3 million accounted for by PRC-related TANF expenditures in SFY 1998.[2] Because state officials view the PRC program as central to their long-run goals, this record has raised concern about the viability of the corporate franchise model, which relies critically on county-level initiative and creativity.

The Origins of Ohio's Approach

After passage of the federal Family Support Act of 1988, Ohio adopted a program called Learning, Earning, and Parenting (LEAP), which targeted case management services to teen parents and pregnant teenagers who were not high school graduates and were not attending school regularly. A combination of financial rewards and sanctions, casework intervention, and childcare services, the program was designed to prevent high school students from dropping out and increase high school graduation rates (Bloom et al., 1993).

When Democratic Governor Richard Celeste proposed LEAP, welfare advocacy groups formed a coalition to protest the initiative as punitive and unfair. County caseworkers who would now be required to fill the education and childcare needs of teen parents were also intensely concerned, as they would have to sanction those not in compliance with the program requirements. LEAP thus provided incentives and penalties, and laid the foundation for coordinated action among those most affected by changes in welfare programs.

When Republican George Voinovich took over as governor in 1991, Ohio was in the midst of a recession and the state was running a budget deficit. Rumor had it that the budget might be balanced by eliminating General Assistance (GA) for single adults without disabilities. Advocates for the poor reactivated to fend off the threatened cuts, forming the Human Services Coalition,[3] joined by the County Commissioners Association. The Human Services Coalition lobbied on behalf of the poor in the legislature and was successful in gaining press attention about the prospect of increased homelessness in the state. This helped convince Democrats in the House to propose an alternative bill, one that created three classes of GA recipients and reduced the amount of support. The Senate, reacting to the lobbying pressure, media attention, and public support, chose to present a modified House version of welfare legislation rather than supporting the governor's proposal. The final result was legislation that established two new state-run programs: Disability Assistance, a program to cover disabled adults and children under age 18, and General Assistance, which provided time-limited cash and medical benefits for single adults.

The defeat of the early Voinovich-supported legislation prompted attacks on the governor for failing to consult with and gain support from legislators and interest groups. The ODHS staff was not consulted on the final version of the bill, and this support typically has been important for passage of welfare-related legislation. One of the enduring outcomes of this effort was a strengthened cooperative arrangement among health and human services interest groups. But the governor had succeeded in elevating the issue of welfare reform and placing it squarely on the legislative agenda.

In 1992 the governor announced that he would establish a blue-ribbon committee composed of a broad coalition of interest groups to help formulate a comprehensive welfare reform plan. But while developing the proposal, the committee discovered that the governor had already drafted a reform blueprint built around the governor's goal of determining and eliminating barriers to employment and self-sufficiency. Coalition members withdrew from the commission, and lacking their support the legislature never seriously considered the legislation. After the false start in 1992, substantive welfare reform took a back seat to other legislative priorities.

In November 1992 the ODHS director resigned, and Voinovich wanted a strong director who shared his vision of welfare reform. In early 1993 he hired Arnold Tompkins, who had been nominated by President Bush to be assistant secretary for management and budget for the U.S. Department of Health and Human Services, and who soon began actively working on welfare proposals. Welfare reform was once again on the legislative agenda. Tompkins became a catalyst for creating a new structure and vision within the department and worked diligently to develop strong relationships with legislative committees. In 1993, the Republican chair of the Senate Ways and Means worked with the governor's office and Director Tompkins to develop legislation proposing a 10-county pilot program to test various aspects of the governor's welfare reform ideas. Although this legislation was not enacted, networks of human service interest groups emerged within several of the more progressive counties that had organized taskforces in anticipation of the pilot program.

1995 Legislation

In 1995 Republicans gained control of both chambers of the legislature, and the chair of the House Human Services Committee worked with the governor's office and ODHS to pass HB 167, signed in August 1995. The bill's title indicated its goal — "to abolish the General Assistance program and make changes in the laws governing ADC." The bill replaced GA benefits for able-bodied childless adults with the Adult Emergency Assistance Program (EAP), which provided one-time payments to meet special needs such as food, clothing, shelter, and transportation that might pose a barrier to employability. The law covered single adults as well as those whose incomes did not exceed 125 percent of federal poverty guidelines. HB 167 also provided money to be passed through from counties to nonprofit agencies serving as emergency food and shelter providers.

But beyond these measures aimed at diverting people from welfare, the primary emphasis of this legislation was on getting people off welfare by preparing them for independence. After Ohio received waivers from the federal guidelines, HB 167 required recipients to participate in jobs and education to retain benefits.[4] The other major change limited the period participants could receive cash assistance to 36 months in any 60-month period. This legislation laid the groundwork for the major changes to result from the federal reform bill.

Federal and State Reform Takes Hold

In August 1996, in response to the passage of TANF, ODHS officials began visiting counties throughout the state and holding public meetings to gain input and support from local constituency groups for the next steps in Ohio's reform process.

In April 1997, the chair of the House Human Services Committee introduced HB 408, which outlined six guiding principles for the state's welfare program: personal responsibility, community involvement, integration of services, simplified service delivery, problem prevention, and evaluation of program outcomes. The most significant change was a shift away from state authority and decision making, with counties given much greater responsibility for designing services for welfare recipients and diverting persons from becoming welfare dependent.

HB 408 passed both houses unanimously — testimony to the work of the governor, the ODHS director, the legislative sponsor, and various welfare advocacy groups. On July 2, 1997, Governor Voinovich signed HB 408 into law.

The Impact of Ohio's Reform on Recipients

The core message of Ohio Works First, as the state's program is called, is that "Ohio has fundamentally changed its welfare system to help people become self-sufficient citizens and take personal responsibility for their own lives and futures. The new system provides temporary services to get people employed and help them stay employed" (ODHS 1996). The emphasis has changed from assessing eligibility and processing checks to assisting in locating employment, training, education, and other support services.

The key institutional element in this program is a shift from central control to "an approach that encourages counties to develop programs based on the needs of their citizens and holds the counties accountable for the outcomes they achieve rather than compliance with federally mandated procedures" (ODHS 1997a). Under OWF, the counties are given much greater flexibility to develop services based on the unique needs of their area.

Prevention, Retention, and Contingency

The counties do this through the Prevention, Retention, and Contingency (PRC) program, which replaces the Emergency Aid Program. PRC is designed to provide temporary assistance to families with at least one child in overcoming immediate barriers to achieving or maintaining self-sufficiency. This effort can take one of three forms. First, PRC can help clients who are in financial crisis avoid OWF rolls in the first place. Second, the program can provide low-income Ohioans with employment and training programs to help them become more employable or progress in their current jobs. Third, PRC can provide services to low-income Ohioans to help them retain their jobs. Each county develops its own PRC program, and can chose to follow the design created by ODHS, modify that design, or develop its own policy.

Each county establishes its own guidelines for PRC eligibility, and these guidelines can be much more flexible than the state's OWF eligibility standards. Most plans fall within a relatively small range: income eligibility in 80 of the 88 counties ranges from 100 percent to 150 percent of federal poverty guidelines, for example. However, one county has established eligibility of up to 200 percent of poverty, while another limits eligibility to 75 percent of poverty.

The maximum assistance available to clients varies from a low of $250 to a high of $2,600 in a 12-month period, with the most common allowance of $1,000 set by 18 counties (ODHS 1998). Twelve of the counties have created a loan fund as part of the PRC program and require repayments once the recipient is employed and able to pay.

The state has created an emergency fund of $5 million each year to allow counties that have experienced a natural disaster to extend and expand their PRC program. In June and July 1998, several

Ohio counties became eligible for emergency funds because of flooding. The only restrictions imposed by the state were that the family have a minor child and have been adversely affected by the flooding.

Benefit Levels and Work Activities

OWF cash grants are based on a combination of income and family size and composition. HB 408 increased cash grants by 6 percent, eliminated the $50 child-support disregard, and gave recipients an earned-income disregard of $250, plus half the additional earned income for 18 months after the client finds work.

For a family unit with only one adult or minor head of household, Ohio requires at least 30 hours of work participation per week. A family unit with two adults is required to work a total of 55 hours per week. OWF allows counties to develop training and developmental programs that serve as alternatives to traditional work for up to 20 percent of their clients. These activities may include parenting classes, alcohol or drug abuse addiction services, counseling for domestic violence victims, and a housing search if the family is homeless. Developmental activities such as school enrollment, adult basic education classes, and post-secondary classes may also count as an allowable alternatives. The state does not have a community service program as part of its OWF menu, but some counties have created sheltered work programs to help clients move into regular employment.

A number of counties have developed unique training and work experience programs. One human service office has taken over a garage and assigns clients to car repair and maintenance classes, to provide them with new skills and teach them how to maintain personal cars for transportation to jobs. Another county has developed a program called Know-How that places women in training programs for apprenticeships in skilled trades. HOST, a program developed in conjunction with the Hotel and Restaurant Operators and a community college, places clients in service jobs in area hotels and restaurants after providing them with basic training. And another county has developed a nurses' aid program that trains clients to become hospice attendants and moves them into nursing homes and hospital care.

Director Tompkins felt strongly about the need for continual development of workforce training programs to encourage clients to move up the income scale and reach greater economic security. To develop such an employment pipeline for clients, ODHS and its Bureau of Workforce Initiatives help counties develop contacts with employers and the business community.[5]

Time Limits

Under H.B. 408, eligible participants can receive cash benefits for up to three years. After reaching the three-year time limit, participants cannot collect cash benefits for at least two years, at which point they can apply for another two years if they need additional assistance and can show good cause why they have been unable to obtain employment. The legislation enumerates a number of situations that can meet the criteria of good cause, including loss of employment, inability to find employment, divorce, domestic violence, and unique personal circumstances. Although the state is experiencing historically low unemployment rates, officials in some rural counties, especially in the southeastern part of the state, where unemployment is still in double-digits, are concerned about what will happen in October 1999 when time limits go into effect.

Sanctions Policy

Ohio has a full-family sanction policy that is administered in a three-tiered, progressive program. First-time failure of a family to comply in full with any provision of the OWF self-sufficiency contract results in the loss of family benefits for one month, or until the family corrects the deficiency. The second failure results in loss of benefits for three payment months, or until the failure ceases, whichever is longer. The third failure to comply ends the group's eligibility for six months.

Each county establishes standards for determining good cause for failure to comply, but the legislation requires each county to eliminate certain barriers to employment. For example, if the county does not fulfill its obligation to assist the client in finding affordable childcare for children under the age of six, the family cannot be sanctioned for failure to comply with work obligations. Even if the family loses benefits through the sanctioning process, a minor child who meets eligibility criteria does not lose medical assistance, even though the adult family member does lose these benefits. In June 1998, 21 percent of case closures had resulted from clients' failure to meet the requirements outlined in their self-sufficiency contracts.

Childcare, Transportation, and Work Incentives

Ohio recognizes that childcare is a necessity for moving custodial parents into the workforce. H.B. 408 originally set the eligibility cap for childcare benefits at 150 percent of poverty, but this was subsequently amended to allow eligibility up to 185 percent of poverty. The legislation allows parents to choose a neighbor, friend, or relative who could provide care, and gives counties responsibility for assisting custodial parents in obtaining the most acceptable childcare available. Early results support the expectation that as welfare rolls decline, the number of children relying on these benefits as a percentage of total OWF children will increase, although the increase has been modest — rising from 8 percent of total OWF children in October 1997 to 9 percent in June 1998.

Each county must also submit a plan that addresses the transportation needs of low-income residents. Counties that are unable to formulate a plan on their own are working with universities or consultants to develop detailed maps of the region that connect welfare clients to employment opportunities.[6] ODHS is also using federal funds to provide counties with technical assistance in developing their transportation plans, and Ohio Department of Transportation officials serve on a task force that is helping counties identify transportation coordinators and design programs to get clients to job and training sites.

Counties are also utilizing PRC funds to purchase gasoline vouchers, bus passes, and car repairs for participants. And three counties have developed "reverse commuting" strategies to help low-income residents of inner-city neighborhoods travel to suburban jobs. Under this program, when public transportation does not exist, the county develops alternative modes to transport clients from the end of bus lines to the job sites (ODHS 1998).

To reward work, Ohio has expanded Medicaid benefits to include children through age 18 in families with earnings under 150 percent of the federal poverty level. This program is simpler than the previous health insurance offered under provisions of the Family Support Act of 1988, because families are not required to visit the County Department of Human Service offices to apply, and recertification is required less frequently.

The Impact of Welfare Reform on Institutions

To support the Work First strategy, Director Tompkins wanted an outcome-based, decentralized organization with cross-functional responsibilities. He selected the franchise model because it allows business franchises to operate independently but with a common mission and core set of activities, and evaluates and rewards them based on key outcome indicators. Under this model, counties develop programs and relationships with service providers that respond to the particular needs and circumstances of their communities. The state, as the franchiser, provides funding, technical support, and training. ODHS also controls product quality — and ensures that programs conform to federal and state statutes — by negotiating a partnership agreement with each county specifying key responsibilities for each party, performance objectives, and evaluation criteria.

To facilitate these changes, the state must adapt to the role of "performance manager" and "coach," while counties must adjust to added flexibility and responsibility.

Partnership Agreements

The cornerstone of the franchise model is the partnership agreement formalizing the relationship between the state and each of Ohio's 88 counties. In the past, the relationship between the two levels of government was established through rules written into the Ohio Administrative Code. The state maintains responsibility for ensuring compliance with federal legislation, but each county now develops specific programs, goals, and objectives for its TANF population.

Before entering a partnership agreement, a county must develop a plan that outlines how it will involve critical community agencies in implementing OWF. The plans are expected to establish connections to employment and training institutions, childcare providers, community drug and alcohol programs, mental health initiatives, and community business and industry leaders. A transportation plan must also be covered in the agreement. Major stakeholders participate in the planning process, and ODHS seeks assurances that the counties will create permanent networks of support agencies and programs to assist clients and break down barriers to long-term employment.

The county obtains fiscal advantages from entering into the partnership agreement, as the state provides a block grant, rather than forwarding 11 funding streams for individual programs. This enables, for example, a county to "transfer money not used for OWF as the caseload declines to provide subsidized childcare for more working families. Pooling funds will also enhance ability to draw down federal funds for some programs."[7]

The consolidated funding and accompanying flexibility also contains a bonus: Counties that meet their objectives and show outstanding achievement are eligible for financial rewards based on set performance measures. These measures include work-activity participation rates and reductions in out-of-wedlock pregnancy. Counties can spend their bonus money on any program benefiting the TANF-eligible population. Counties establishing partnership agreements early had a distinct advantage in obtaining bonus payments, as a smaller number of counties divided a set amount of money.

The Key Role of State Account Managers

The account manager's job is central to the concept of the franchise model. Each of 12 ODHS account managers is responsible for a designated region within Ohio and serves as a liaison between the county and the state. The primary role of these account managers is to help counties succeed in meeting the performance objectives established in the partnership agreements. Account managers download state case management reports, assist with integrated information management systems, help counties develop reports for the state, provide training programs, conduct and publicize local conferences and community outreach programs, and keep counties informed of resources available from the state and federal government, foundations, and other sources. The account managers meet regularly in Columbus to keep abreast of new programs, technology upgrades, and state and federal legislative changes.

Account managers also maintain regular contact with local development and employment boards, and attend training sessions through the Ohio Department of Development enabling them to connect human service clients with business and training programs. The state also anticipates that account managers will develop teams of people and programs who work on a continuous process improvement model to help build on strengths and overcome weaknesses.

Management Information Systems

Counties have voiced widespread concern about the state's management information system (MIS). This concern was addressed in Temporary Law Section 15, which required ODHS to consult with counties and develop a plan for addressing technological support. While a preliminary assessment has been completed, work on this plan, and on the development of an integrated MIS system for assessing performance, is ongoing.

Like many other states, Ohio realized a budget surplus under the new federal welfare reform, and the state is using a substantial portion of these funds to enhance its management information capabilities. The goal is to develop an integrated tracking system to facilitate automated case management. Ohio now has six major information systems in place or under development to track client information, including the Client Registry Information System — Enhanced, the Support Enforcement Tracking System, the Medicaid Management Information System, the Family and Children Services Information System, the Day Care Reporting System, and the Statewide Automated Child Welfare Information System.

A new system — the Integrated Client Management System — will integrate components of the existing systems and allow counties and ODHS to "slice and dice" the data for more flexible use and interpretation. Linking these data and providing them to account managers for purposes of assessing county progress in meeting performance objectives is a top priority. The integrated MIS system will require not only hardware and software but also staff training. And issues concerning data access, privacy, formatting, and data retention make for a complicated set of policy questions that must be negotiated between the state and counties as well as among a variety of state agencies.

Evaluation Studies

Early on, Director Tompkins established an Office of Research and Long-Term Planning to evaluate ODHS efforts and to provide strategic planning advice for the director and the legislature. Much of the work was contracted out to universities and private consulting firms. For example, MACRO, a consulting firm in Princeton, N.J., is conducting a four-year project to evaluate OWF policy, process, and outcomes. Ohio State University is conducting an 18-month study of closed welfare cases that will serve as a guide to longer-term tracking of OWF recipients. More recently, the Taft administration has combined the state Office of Research and Technology and the Office of Internal Audits into the newly created Office of Research, Evaluation, and Accounting. A division of research will continue evaluation projects with oversight provided by a newly created research council composed of state officials and private and university policy analysts and researchers.

How ODHS Collaborates with Other State Agencies

In the past, ODHS has contracted with a number of state agencies to perform specific services for the County Human Services Departments (CDHS). For example, ODHS contracted with the Ohio Department of Education (ODOE) to provide classroom and technical training for welfare recipients. To fund this effort, ODHS forwarded funds from the federal AFDC program to ODOE, which contributed the required state match. The latter then contracted with the counties for services. When these contracts expired at the end of 1997, ODHS decided to pass TANF funds directly to the counties, which decide how best to offer training and other services. In the case of continuing education services, for example, a county can now decide to contract with retired schoolteachers or with local school districts.

ODHS still has a number of formal interagency agreements, but these are non-funded guidelines intended to promote interagency coordination. For example, ODHS has such an agreement with the Ohio Department of Development covering staff training on employment opportunities for economically vulnerable individuals, and negotiations with businesses regarding the hiring and retraining of economically vulnerable individuals.

TANF Employment and Training

When the U.S. Department of Labor's Welfare-to-Work (WTW) program announced that it would be awarding grants, plans called for the money to be administered through OBES. A number of concerns about the requirements of the grant surfaced immediately, and ultimately Governor Voinovich decided not to apply for WTW money. In a letter to Secretary of Labor Alexis Herman, he cited the "funding eligibility and information reporting" requirements as inconsistent with Ohio's approach to serve the TANF population. Instead the state developed its own program using unobligated TANF money.

To move hard-to-serve clients into work within the state's three-year welfare time limit, ensure continued employment, and enhance participants' ability to increase their earnings, Ohio developed a TANF Employment and Training (TANF E&T) program funded by $44 million of TANF funds earmarked for FY 1999 and FY 2000. This program targets people on assistance for 24 months or longer, as well as clients who have the characteristics of long-term dependency, such as teen mothers, individuals with multiple barriers to work, and individuals without a high school diploma or equivalency certification. Each county health services department must submit a plan to serve this population, coordinate among local agencies, and set targeted goals before receiving TANF E&T funds. These plans must also demonstrate how the new program builds on the One-Stop initiative being undertaken by OBES. Funds are then distributed to the county commissioners, who contract for services through the health serviced department, Private Industry Council (PIC), or an alternative service provider. The funds can be used to provide employment services, placement services, and post-employment job retention activities.

TANF Early Start

A collaboration with the Ohio Department of Health is designed to help stabilize families so that they can be prepared to work when their children's ages permit. This prevention program provides home visits, parent education, and early screenings for at-risk infants, as well as referrals to other services. As with the TANF E&T program, the counties receive funds earmarked from federal TANF funds for children's programs. The county departments of human services are encouraged to work with Family and Children First Councils and Ohio's Early Start program to provide guidance for the programs.[8] By autumn 1998, the program covered all 88 counties and was funded with $28 million of TANF money.

Other Agencies

Among other cooperative efforts, the Bureau of Motor Vehicles helps ODHS locate absent parents who are delinquent with child-support payments. An interagency agreement with the Department of Transportation also coordinates local efforts to remove transportation barriers to employment. Again, the money is distributed through the counties, which control the way these programs work. Cooperative programs also exist with the Department of Alcohol and Drug Addiction Services and the Department of Health for preventing and treating alcohol and drug-related problems. Counties choose from menus of services for their clients when deciding how best to meet their mandated goals. For example, Lucas County stations a drug and alcohol clinician in its human service offices to do assessments and assist clients.

These partnerships with other state agencies have not always gone smoothly. Attempts to work with OBES were fraught with difficulty, for example, partly because of different agency perceptions about core missions and client populations. OBES sees its client base as employers and people with recent attachment to the labor force and good employment prospects, while ODHS sees its clients as needing training or assistance before they join the labor force. These problems have manifested themselves in a reluctance to share computer information: OBES is not connected to ODHS's information system, so requests for data can take weeks or months. Organizationally, OBES operates as a state system through regional offices, while ODHS has moved to a highly decentralized 88-county system, and this further complicates relations. One of the first major policy initiatives under Governor Robert Taft has been the proposed merger of these two agencies into the Department of Job and Family Services. This follows a period during the Voinovich administration that one very knowledgeable observer describes as one of "white hot friction" between the two agencies. Scheduled to occur by January 2000, this merger will require overcoming what are generally described as significant cultural differences between the two agencies and the rewriting of over 200 pages of state law.

Making Devolution Work — A Tale of Two Counties

Two of Ohio's largest urban counties, Hamilton (Cincinnati) and Franklin (Columbus), were among the first to restructure their operations. Their experiences provide insight into the sharp differences emerging in how counties are responding to the challenges and opportunities under TANF.

These differences emerge even though the two counties are similar in their workforce composition, income, unemployment, and education levels, and both tend to elect more Republican than Democratic representatives (see Table 1).

Franklin County operates in a fragmented human services environment, with income maintenance, child welfare, and child support operating under separate administrative structures. Successful case management depends critically on cooperation among a wide variety of human service agencies.

Franklin County has made a substantial investment in moving operations into the neighborhoods, with plans to create five Community Opportunity Centers (COC), each of which will offer a full range of TANF-related services. The first COC opened in spring 1998 in a renovated shopping center on the south side of town. Personnel from Franklin County Children Services and Child Support Enforcement have been stationed at the center to expedite referrals. Another important agency, the Franklin County Alcohol and Drug Abuse and Mental Health Board (ADAMH), does not station

Table 1		
	Franklin	*Hamilton*
County Profile	Location: Central Ohio Major city: Columbus Unemployment: 2.5% (1998) Population: Over 1 million Industries: State government, university, and services. AFDC participation rate of 7% (state average 6%), with extensive pockets of concentrated poverty.	Location: SW Corner of the state Major city: Cincinnati Unemployment: 3.6 % (1998) Population: .86 million Industries: Manufacturing, services. AFDC participation rate of 7%, with pockets of concentrated poverty.
Social Service Program Structure	Fragmented system of service delivery, with income maintenance, child support enforcement, children services, and JTPA under separate administrative structures.	Triple-combined system, with child welfare, income maintenance, child support enforcement under one management structure. JTPA also housed in the Hamilton County Department of Human Services (HCDHS).
Office Location	Decentralized operation with Community Opportunity Centers (COC) to be located in neighborhoods and central administration located downtown.	Central location in downtown Cincinnati.
Case Management Approach	Total case management system, with case managers trained in all areas of income maintenance, food stamp, mentoring and support services. Representatives of referral agencies out-stationed within the COC.	Team approach to service delivery. Caseworkers part of an Integrated Strategic Business Unit (ISBU), which contains a team leader, technical service advisor, clerical worker, and caseworkers from income maintenance, child support enforcement, and children services, plus a daycare coordinator.
Prevention, Retention, Contingency Program	Adopted a modified state model, with income standard set at 150% of federal poverty guidelines (FPG) and yearly assistance limited to $500. PRC services provided through the Franklin County Department of Human Services.	Adopted its own PRC model, with income standards set at 150% FPG, and yearly assistance available through both the HCDHS (up to $300 per client) and through a contract arrangement with a consortium of community-based organizations (up to $900 per client).

personnel at the center, so referrals for such services must be made outside the COCs.

Hamilton County, in contrast, organizes caseworkers into integrated strategic business units organized by Zip codes. The teams include income maintenance, child-support, and children services workers, and this arrangement substantially reduces the complexities of coordinating referrals among a variety of agencies. However, Hamilton County is investing much less in neighborhood outreach and has chosen to continue operations from a centralized downtown location.

The two counties also differ markedly in the design of their Prevention, Retention, and Contingency programs. Franklin County has adopted a modified state model, making annual one-time payments up to $500 per client. Hamilton County, on the other hand, is widely credited with having one of the most innovative PRC programs, with extensive involvement by community organizations aimed at diverting persons from needing OWF assistance and ensuring that they do not need to return. Under the Family Boost program, the county provides direct assistance when clients need limited emergency funds up to $300. When the family crisis is more complex, the county contracts with ACT, a community consortium of social service agencies, to provide resources to keep the family off welfare for at least three months. The service provider negotiates an additional in-depth personal responsibility agreement with the participant, and can terminate PRC services if the participant fails to abide by the agreement.

Overall, Franklin County has a fragmented system, while Hamilton County has established teams organized to integrate a full array of services according to the specific needs of each family. Hamilton County's PRC program is much more decentralized than that of Franklin County. Both counties are moving toward neighborhood-based service units — Franklin by locating service centers in neighborhoods, and Hamilton by creating teams to work with clients from the same neighborhoods.

Despite their differences, employees in both Franklin and Hamilton Counties have voiced skepticism about the sincerity of mid-level state bureaucrats in devolving authority to counties. One example concerns workforce development, where the state has organized meetings between counties and local employers to encourage communication and information sharing with potential employees. The larger counties feel they are better able to organize efforts that respond to their needs.

Both counties view advocacy by ODHS account managers as important in obtaining state support and resources, and express concern that account managers may not be given the tools and the authority necessary to best serve county needs. In Hamilton, for example, county representatives thought they had negotiated a valid partnership agreement with the ODHS team, but after the state reviewed the plan it required the county to renegotiate some sections. Thus, while counties were told that the negotiating team would have the authority to finalize the agreement, this authority turned out to be subject to higher-level approval.

Most significantly, the counties are skeptical about the state's ability to upgrade its technology to support and reward local reform and give counties the reliable information and flexibility they want. Recognizing some of the limits the state faces in developing new information systems, counties are creating partnerships to provide expanded MIS services to each other, especially between some of the larger urban counties and smaller rural counties. Counties are also advising each other on how to use the state system more efficiently.

County-to-County Partnerships

Counties are collaborating in other ways as well. A group of smaller counties in the northern and central part of the state organized a conference on the changing role of the county departments of human services. Given drastically reduced caseloads, preventive services under PRC may soon become the dominant program activity for these counties. The conference as well as a follow-up meeting addressed the challenges of serving a smaller but more difficult population, as well as opportunities for enlarging the voice of smaller counties in the policy process.

The state recognizes the expertise that counties are developing and is using that knowledge by engaging county administrators in the state planning process. A taskforce called Voice of the Customer convened line and supervisory personnel from half a dozen counties to help ODHS define MIS system needs, and to identify areas for better data collection and analysis.

The Role of Community-Based Organizations and the Way Forward

While Ohio's reform effort is designed to devolve responsibility to the counties, the state is also interested in seeing counties devolve programs to community-based organizations. Counties that follow this more decentralized model are being touted as "best practice" examples. The state has also demonstrated its willingness to directly contract with community-based organizations if individual counties do not. For example, ODHS has established pilot projects with local neighborhood and faith-based community organizations at a cost of $7.7 million. These projects target hard-to-serve participants or demonstrate innovative approaches for moving TANF-eligible populations into the workplace.

One such project, EXODUS, is a faith-based program in Cincinnati that helps OWF participants deal with every aspect of job readiness. The program includes vocational assessments and classes in budgeting and housekeeping. Extensively trained members of participating congregations pair with OWF families for one year to provide support services. ODHS and EXODUS sponsored a statewide conference on welfare reform and faith-based organizations to provide ideas on job retention and job readiness, and to encourage such surrogate support systems.

The state also supports the Cleveland Urban League's job readiness program in the Carl B. Stokes Social Services mall, located in a housing development where more than half of the residents are OWF participants. The Urban League has partnered with several major employers to secure job training, apprenticeships, and employment opportunities for OWF participants.

Similarly, Greenbriar Community Enrichment Center in Columbus has established a grassroots training program for OWF participants that focuses on job readiness, job placement, and motivation, as well childcare and prevention of domestic violence.

These and other state-funded programs are being promoted as models for involving community-based organizations in local reform efforts. The state has reinforced this focus by offering $5 million in funding for community-based groups that the counties will administer in partnership with them. Over 200 community organizations applied for this funding, of which 44 received grants.

Such partnerships, and the ability and willingness of counties to develop them, will be the key to the next stage of reform in Ohio. With the clear shift in emphasis toward keeping people off welfare, community-based organizations are critical to the success of welfare reform in Ohio. Prevention is difficult in a highly centralized, state-run system — it takes a county. But unless counties are willing to break out of bureaucratic mindsets and engage the broader community in identifying the need for preventive services and participating in their delivery, devolution will merely substitute one remote bureaucracy for another.

Other factors that will play a critical role and warrant future review include leadership within ODHS. The former director was clearly a guiding force in his belief in welfare reform and the need to devolve authority to community-based organizations. Early in his first term, Governor Taft announced the appointment of Jacqui Romer Sensky as the director of human services. Ms. Sensky was a deputy chief of staff for Governor Voinovich who had worked with both the legislature and the previous director to set the welfare reform agenda in Ohio. With this appointment, changes begun under the last administration are expected to continue in the same direction.

At the management level, the shift from state to local control depends on the role of the newly created ODHS account manager. Because these managers were hired late, the success of this critical link between the state and ODHS operations is not yet clear.

Organizationally, action was taken in the last legislative secession to create a single state department to oversee employment and family services. Governor Taft endorsed this concept, and the Department of Job and Family Services will be created by merging ODHS and OBES by July 2000. Combining these two structures will pose challenges for continued devolution of welfare reform in Ohio. Each agency is organized very differently — ODHS is decentralized, with 88 county-run programs, while OBES is a state-administered system operating through a network of regional offices. Top officials in both departments are quick to point out significant cultural differences between the two — one geared to the employment needs of the long-term unemployed, and the other to the needs of a developed workforce and Ohio's business community.

For their part, welfare clients and their advocates may mount a legal challenge if county programs differ too much. Should that happen, the state may become more reluctant to allow counties as much flexibility as they now have, and counties may feel compelled to request more guidance from the state.

Yet overall, counties are responding positively to their additional responsibilities and would likely oppose any effort to restrict their roles. Despite the inevitable changes in and challenges to the state's new welfare program as it matures, Ohio is unlikely to return soon to its earlier rule-driven human services model, and will continue to push for creative community-based problem solving.

References

Bloom, Dan, Veronica Fellerath, David Long, and Robert Wood. 1993. *LEAP: Interim Findings on a Welfare Initiative to Improve School Attendance Among Teenage Parents: Ohio's Learning, Earning, and Parenting Program.* New York: Manpower Demonstration Research Corp.

Fook, Jan. 1996. The Reflective Researcher: Developing a Reflective Approach to Practice, In *The Reflective Researcher*, Jan Fook, ed., Sydney, Australia: Allen & Unwin Pty Ltd.

Governor Voinovich Does Not Apply for $88 Million Federal Welfare to Work Grant, Says State. http://www.state.oh.us/obes/html.welfare_to_work.htm.

Governor Signs Historic Welfare Reform Legislation. 1997 (July 2). http://www.state.oh.us/odhs/releases/rl070297.htm.

Governor Announces Human Services Director. 1999 (February 2). http://www.state.oh.us/odhs/releases/rl/022699.

Hough, Gary. 1996. Using Ethnographic Methods to Research the Work World of Social Workers in Child Protection. In *The Reflective Researcher*. Jan Fook, ed., Sydney, Australia: Allen & Unwin Pty Ltd.

Ohio Department of Human Services. 1999. County Prevention, Retention, and Contingency Programs, March. http://www.ohio.gov/odhs/owf/prc/prc0399.htm.

Ohio Department of Human Services. Franklin County Partnership Agreement. http://www.ohio.gov/odhs.owf/partagre/franklin/index.HTM.

Ohio Department of Human Services. Hamilton County Partnership Agreement. http://www.ohio.gov/odhs.owf/partagre/hamilton/index.HTM.

Ohio Department of Human Services. 1998. Ohio Works First: For Our Future, Our Families, Our Businesses, Our Communities. Columbus, OH: Department of Human Services, September 16.

Ohio Department of Human Services. 1997a. *Ohio Works First Retreat*, Vols. 1 and 2. Columbus, OH: Department of Human Services, July 17-18.

Ohio Department of Human Services. 1997b. Quick Reference of OWF Changes to Impact Counties, October 1. http://www.ohio.gov/odhs/owf/colett/octone03.html.

One Stop Shop of South Central Ohio. http://www.bright.net/~osssco/home.html.

Sheridan, R.G. 1995. Politics and Welfare Reform Don't Mix in Ohio. In *The Politics of Welfare Reform*, ed. by Donald F. Norris and Lyke Thompson, Thousand Oaks: Sage Publications.

Endnotes

1   According to a December 1998 DHHS-ACF report, the TANF work participation rate in Ohio met the federal standard for all families, but, as was the case for the majority of states, the 39.8 percent rate for two-parent families was below the adjusted standard of 47.8 percent. (Http://www.acf. dhhs.gov/programs/opre/particip/pprate97.htm).

2   Ohio's fiscal calendar runs from July 1 to June 30. In FY '98, only nine months of the initial PRC program dollars were covered as the program did not go into effect until October 1, 1997.

3   The Human Service Coalition included most major religious organizations, organizations representing children's advocacy groups, organizations that help the homeless, and other major social service organizations. Once organized, this coalition continued to be a strong presence in the legislative process throughout the passage of H.B. 167 and H.B. 408.

4   Examples of workplace and training programs in HB 167 included daycare subsidies and credits; enhanced support services for families through Head Start, WIC and subsidized meal programs at schools; retention of greater portions of the payments received through child support orders for families on public assistance; drug screening programs for pregnant women and mandatory drug and alcohol addiction counseling for those who test positive; pilot programs in counties testing an electronic transfer food stamp system; and a new training program for non-custodial parents with the aim of increasing child support collections.

5   "Ohio Work First for Our Future," Progress Report, Ohio Department of Human Services, September 16, 1998. The pipeline concept was first introduced to counties during early meetings between citizens and ODHS officials.

6   Several of the Appalachian counties are using the services of the Institute for Local Government and Rural Development associated with Ohio University to develop these maps.

7   "Overview: Ohio-Hamilton County Human Services Partnership Agreement," Hamilton County Department of Human Services, 1998.

8   The Ohio Family and Children First initiative is an umbrella organization that coordinates services from diverse organizations to promote better service delivery to families and children.

Chapter 3

KANSAS CARVES OUT A MIDDLE GROUND

Jocelyn M. Johnston and Kara Lindaman

Kansas policymakers have made fundamental changes in the state's welfare program, but both elected officials and the bureaucracy have done so in a fashion consistent with the state's dominant political and administrative culture: cautiously and incrementally.

Indeed, one preliminary study of how states are positioned in the early reform period places Kansas squarely in the middle (American Public Welfare Association 1997). Rather than becoming more penurious toward its welfare recipients, Kansas has followed the lead of several other states and redrawn the parameters with which its welfare population is to be defined. From the perspective of welfare administrators, caseloads will now consist of households led by adults who are preparing for work and independence. The state provides a foundation of support for a household's pre-independence status, including treatment for substance abuse, childcare and transportation assistance, and emergency and short-term housing assistance. The state also invests in programs designed to help the adult secure and sustain employment. Pure income support is reserved for a small portion of households judged incapable of full independence.

There is little evidence to suggest that Kansas will engage in an interstate race to the bottom: Although the welfare program has shifted to a work-first philosophy, it has not substantially altered financial eligibility or cash benefit levels.[1] Indeed, for most components of the state's Temporary Assistance for Families (TAF) program (the Kansas version of the federal TANF), the state has opted to be as generous as the federal government allows, and as generous as most other states. Overall, Kansas now spends more per recipient than before its reform efforts.

Adults in TAF households are expected to participate in up to 40 hours of job-related activities per week, and most applicants must complete a mandatory job search to qualify for benefits. Eligibility is no longer determined by a separate caseworker. Instead, caseworkers use an integrated approach that includes a focus on employment or employment preparation activities. Essentially, the state opted to shift emphasis from education and training for welfare recipients to short-term, skills-specific training. Welfare administrators were familiar with research suggesting that such a shift would place recipients in jobs more quickly (Gueron and Pauly 1991; Riccio, Friedlander, and Freedman 1994). Regional and national meetings such as those offered by the American Public Welfare Association (APWA) and exchanges with other state administrators also led Kansas to espouse the work-first view of welfare. Kansas administrators were particularly impressed with work-first policies adopted in Utah and Oregon. Kansas has also added teeth to its sanctions policy, suspending benefits to the entire household in the event of non-compliance with the new TAF requirements.

Between 1993 and 1997, Kansas saw a 43 percent reduction in its AFDC caseload (U.S. Department of Health and Human Services 1998) — the fourteenth largest during that period, according to Gais, Boyd, and Davis (1997). These reductions occurred despite the absence of drastic policy shifts such as those adopted in Michigan, Minnesota, and Wisconsin (Wiseman 1996). The central plains economy was improving throughout this period, which explains part of the caseload reduction. An official at the Kansas Department of Social and Rehabilitation Services (SRS), which administers the welfare program, has offered a demographic explanation: declining birth rates and the relatively slow rate of growth in the state's young female population.

Tufts University's Center on Poverty and Hunger ranks Kansas near the bottom with regard to its investment in TANF (Tufts 1998), but the study drew erroneous conclusions about some features of the state's welfare policy.[2] An SRS-corrected score would give the state a ranking of 30th (tied with four other states), as opposed to the Tufts ranking of 49th (Kansas SRS, 1998b) — consistent with the typical Kansas position in rankings of state social welfare programs.[3] It is highly unlikely that the Kansas legislature will ignore the needs of families that reach the mandatory federal TANF five-year limit; when push comes to shove, the state will assist these families with state-only funds.

The Politics of Program Design in Kansas

The Kansas approach to welfare reform stems from a combination of executive leadership, strong public and political consensus, and relatively weak interest groups. The state's fiscally conservative but socially moderate tradition, and the leadership of moderate Republican Governor Bill Graves, paved the way for administrative domination of welfare reform. With the exception of strong disagreements surrounding enforcement of child support, the legislature — long dominated by the Republican Party — and interest groups have mounted only muted resistance to welfare policy initiatives.

Welfare reform in Kansas has been consistent with the state's approach to change in other social welfare domains (Johnston and Lindaman, 1998; Johnston, Davis and Fox, 1998): policy movement is often framed by careful review of programs in Kansas and in other states,[4] and by relatively low levels of conflict.[5] The absence of dramatic change has further minimized conflict — in sharp contrast to Wisconsin where a change from very generous welfare support to a much more stringent policy attracted a great deal of attention.

Although the current governor cannot be considered entrepreneurial in the sense of Governor Tommy Thompson of Wisconsin, Governor Graves facilitated a reform environment that precluded vigorous legislative intervention, despite the potential for strong challenges from the more conservative members of his Republican party. That environment included the leadership of an SRS secretary who had served for seventeen years in the Kansas legislature, including service as chair of the House Appropriations Committee. The secretary's understanding of legislators' expectations, and her ability to rally staff around crucial policy decisions, has curtailed conflict between legislators and the social welfare bureaucracy. The secretary was also known as a critic of SRS during her legislative career, further blunting potential conservative legislative criticism: She was viewed as someone who could improve the agency. The secretary's leadership of a 35 percent downsizing of SRS further helped reduce legislative criticism of the "monster" agency (Myers 1997). The combined efforts of the governor, the SRS secretary, and her staff laid the foundation for a moderate response to the discretion for state initiative provided by the 1996 Personal Responsibility and Work Opportunity Reconciliation Act (PRWORA).

Governor Graves has also espoused an aggressive strategy for reducing the size of SRS that resulted in reviews of most SRS commissions and subsequent privatization of a number of functions, including child-support enforcement, foster care, adoptions, family preservation activities, and an array of Medicaid services for elderly and disabled individuals. Many of these initiatives entailed awarding contracts to nonprofit agencies, or "non-profitization" (Nathan 1997a; Nathan and Gais 1998). These privatization/non-profitization contracts have been plagued by familiar problems: an inadequate supply of providers, insufficient monitoring of contracts, and questionable cost-saving potential (Johnston and Romzek 1999; Romzek and Johnston 1999; State of Kansas 1995). Nonetheless, by convincing legislators that he had effectively shrunk SRS, the governor was able to head off the most conservative wings of his party and minimize resistance to the influence of SRS in reforming welfare.

One politically contentious reform issue did lead to legislative conflict with the governor: the child-support enforcement features of PRWORA, which require all employers to report information concerning new hires to a designated state agency. Matches between this information and files from the child-support enforcement unit then facilitate collection of child-support payments. This system was the subject of significant legislative controversy, including vocal opposition from the most conservative wings. A primary concern voiced by one group is the right to individual privacy. Lawmakers ultimately authorized state compliance with federal requirements, but also stipulated that the state file suit against the federal government.[6]

Recent program refinements in the state's welfare program underscore its traditional moderate social policy stance. For example, the legislature did not agree to a proposed increase in the TAF earned income disregard from 40 percent to 50 percent. But its decision was motivated in part by recognition that a 50 percent policy may lengthen recipient TAF enrollment, thereby imposing future hardships on some clients as they reach their 60-month benefit time limit more quickly. Similarly, the state decided to provide $40 monthly payments to all TAF families receiving child support, allocating roughly $3.7 million for these grants in fiscal year 1999 from the state's general fund. These grants replaced the loss of $50 in federal benefits faced by TANF families receiving child support.

Kansas has not enacted new welfare laws since passage of the 1996 federal legislation, with the exception of provisions designed to authorize compliance with federal child-support enforcement requirements. Instead, administrative action is loosely guided by 1994 legislation authorizing *KanWork*, the Kansas version of JOBS, as well as an SRS application for a waiver from federal AFDC requirements.[7] Because of impending federal reforms, the U.S. Department of Health and Human Services (HHS) and Kansas opted against formal approval of the waiver, choosing instead to have most of the waiver application provisions grandfathered into the Kansas TANF plan.

The Role of Interest Groups

In the months leading up to reform, as the implementation of KanWork progressed and the state formulated its response to PRWORA, SRS leaders fanned out across the state to host community forums designed to solicit input from local leaders, advocacy and other interest groups, and citizens. These forums generated relatively low levels of conflict and allowed top welfare administrators to diffuse potential dissension.[8]

Although welfare advocacy groups resisted some aspects of the new policies, they have garnered little support, in part because of legislative and bureaucratic policy consensus. Two groups dominate traditional welfare advocacy in the state. One consists of a non-denominational consortium of churches that lobbies the legislature. The second group consists of leaders of programs that use local volunteers to offer support for welfare mothers.

During the policy reform process, the state did rely on input from the KanWork Interagency Council, which included representatives from state departments of Commerce and Housing, Human Resources, and Education, as well as private employers, childcare and other welfare advocacy groups, and clients.[9] The council continues to function as an advisory group to SRS.

The participation of interest groups in community forums, the KanWork Interagency Council, and welfare task forces might be expected to lead to friendly, informal contacts between advocates and SRS officials, but most such contacts remain relatively formal. Most interest groups have requested information and policy modifications through the legislative committee charged with monitoring the implementation of welfare reform.[10]

Early in 1998, SRS asked food banks throughout Kansas — the traditional advocates for the poor — whether welfare reforms had increased people's need for donated food and meals. Almost all reported relatively little change in their client's needs, and several also voiced support for the state's new welfare policies and work requirements (Kansas Department of Social and Rehabilitation Services 1998a).

The Design Components of TAF

Like most other states, Kansas has adopted a work-first philosophy as a foundation of its TAF program, and has imposed a 60-month time limit on cash benefits. The state has also made an explicit decision to invest in services designed to secure employment for adults needing welfare. In the words of a top SRS welfare administrator, Kansas has opted to shift to a "tough love" approach.

Kansas welfare programs are formally centralized, but 12 regional state offices deliver services throughout the state. These regional offices, known as local area offices, or LAOs, have substantial administrative and policy discretion over various elements of TAF. For example, LAOs have the authority to enter into provider agreements, most of which are used to offer the employment services considered critical to the success of the new program.

Job Search, Training, and Other Employment Services

The new work emphasis embodied in TAF begins with a job search required of non-exempt applicants before they can receive benefits.[11] Caseworkers can grant exemptions if an applicant is a teenage in-school parent, faces severe barriers to employment (including poor local economic conditions), or is a female head of household in her third trimester of pregnancy. Exempt applicants must participate in an employment assessment program, which intensifies after cash assistance actually begins. For non-exempt applicants, the job search entails up to 25 hours of activities that include completion of applications and group activities designed to help the applicant secure employment, as well as weekly contact with the caseworker.

Each LAO has substantial discretion over the job search requirements. In some LAOs, caseworkers perform random checks of job search activity by checking with employers to verify that a welfare client submitted an application. If the caseworker is satisfied that the applicant is making a good faith effort and has completed other portions of eligibility determination, then the applicant may receive cash benefits before completing the job search. Other LAOs require applicants to complete the 25-hour job search before receiving cash assistance. Some LAOs contract with local governmental, private, or nonprofit organizations to administer the job searches.

Although the mandatory job search has been characterized as a diversion by some critics (Vobejda and Havemann 1998), SRS officials indicate that most applicants complete their search well within the normal ten days that caseworkers require to complete the eligibility determination process. Nonetheless, the mandatory job search sends a clear anti-dependency signal to the client. Kansas SRS officials also respond that they operate none of the programs that other states use to keep people off welfare, such as one-time emergency cash grants.

After the TAF applicant qualifies for cash assistance, Kansas requires up to 40 hours per week of continued employment-related activity for TAF beneficiaries (55 hours per week for two-parent households). As with the initial job search, most LAOs contract with local governmental, nonprofit, and private agencies for "employment preparation services" (EPS), such as adult basic education, job development, job training, and job placement activities. Education and long-term training are used sparingly. Kansas does not provide TAF community-service jobs but does include a small "work experience" component, in which recipients are employed by nonprofit and public organizations. Several arrangements also exist between LAOs and private employers. One visible example is Cessna Aircraft's 21st Street program, located in Wichita, which provides job training and jobs for TAF clients. From 1990 to 1997 Cessna trained over 250 welfare recipients for well-paid jobs. When President Clinton visited Wichita in November 1997 he hailed the 21st Street program as a "model for the nation" (McLean 1997).

Early in 1997 SRS informed the legislature's SRS Transition Oversight Committee that it would incorporate recommendations from advocacy groups concerning TAF-required employment activities. Advocates had voiced reservations about the stringent nature of Kansas' 90-day work-first requirement, which stipulates that all TAF adults must participate in a job search, job readiness, or work experience activity within 90 days of receiving assistance. The advocates focused on TAF adults who lack employment skills. Because job training is not offered during the first 90 days, the advocates argued, the system was unfair to women who are unskilled and who require training to compete in the labor market. In response to these concerns, adults with poor work histories and low skill levels were offered job training within the first 90 days of assistance. Caseworkers were also authorized to waive the 90-day work-first requirement if, in their opinion, the combination of the local labor market and the recipient's skill level indicated little chance of securing employment.

More recently, SRS has shortened the work-first period to 60 days but has also provided more work exemptions, and is intensifying employment preparation services for those with substantial barriers to employment. This intensification stems in part from the state's concern that not all clients with serious employment barriers can be accommodated in the federally mandated 20 percent caseload limit for exemptions from work requirements. Because some of these recipients could fall victim to the 60-month TANF time limit, SRS is strengthening employment services in an effort to move them into employment.

A number of state agencies, including the departments of Corrections and Commerce and Housing, as well as the Rehabilitation Services Commission of SRS, have been enlisted in the effort to address specific employment needs. For example, the Rehabilitation Services Commission of SRS works with TAF clients — especially long-term recipients or those who frequently require welfare assistance — on job-related skills. SRS officials characterize their relationship with the Rehabilitation Services Commission as "innovative," and indeed, at a recent regional TANF-vocational education conference, few states claimed a comparable working relationship. In addition, SRS and Corrections have designed a protocol for newly released prisoners, many of whom are women who turn to TAF for support, and many of whom require treatment for substance abuse to obtain and maintain employment. The Department of Commerce and Housing, represented on the KanWork Interagency Council and other groups working to enhance opportunities for TAF clients, hosts sessions on TAF employment and training at public housing sites.

Under KanWork, SRS was required to enter statewide agreements with the Kansas Department of Human Resources (KDHR, the counterpart to other states' departments of labor), to provide some employment-related services. These agreements proved to be somewhat antagonistic. According to one LAO director, because KDHR's performance was evaluated based on job placements, the agency had relatively little reason to devote resources to hard-core unemployed AFDC recipients. Today, however, SRS works closely with KDHR to fashion employment services for TAF recipients, and the LAO director believes that the new SRS-KDHR relationship will be far more successful.

In addition to these linkages, SRS is working closely with Rehabilitation Services, Corrections, the University of Kansas, and a variety of other organizations to refine a tool for diagnosing learning disabilities. Designed as part of a national pilot program, this tool will be used to help assess clients' employability with the intention of providing intervention and treatment for applicants identified as learning disabled. Participation in treatment programs will be counted as qualified employment activity.

Sanctions

Under previous policy, Kansas reduced household benefits only partially if an adult in the household failed to comply with AFDC program requirements; cash benefits continued for other members of the household. But as of 1997, a new full-family sanction policy terminates all cash benefits for the household if an adult does not comply with TAF requirements. During the last months of 1997, two of the state's welfare advocacy groups requested that the legislature's SRS Transition Oversight Committee assess this new sanction policy.

The SRS secretary's testimony on the issue at the beginning of the 1998 legislative session confirmed interview data collected as part of the State Capacity Study. Essentially, SRS administrators and caseworkers supported the full-family sanction policy, in part because they viewed it as more humane than the previous partial sanction policy. In the past, sanctioned families made do with their reduced grants, riding out the partial sanction period, and SRS staff felt that the policy had no teeth and that children suffered as a result. SRS officials report that heads of TAF households are far more likely to avoid full-family sanctions, so children are actually better off.

The SRS secretary testified that prior to the full-family policy, 20 percent of TANF cases were under sanction at any point in time. Under the new policy, sanctioned cases tend to account for less than 3 percent of all TAF cases, and second-time sanctions constitute less than .2 percent of all cases. Under the new policy, clients facing first-time sanction can reopen their cases immediately upon complying with work requirements. Later sanctions require benefit suspension for a minimum of two months.[12] For the time being, at least, there is no substantial conflict between the legislature and state administrators around this policy, despite the opposition of welfare advocacy groups.

Transportation, Childcare, and Other Support Services

Transportation and childcare services are viewed as critical components of the state's efforts to foster employment and independence for TAF clients. Resources devoted to these support services are relatively fluid, with signals from the state that LAOs are free — indeed encouraged — to provide generous support in these areas. As in other states, the Kansas welfare program is spending more per case under TANF than under AFDC, and much of this spending is directed to work-support services such as transportation and childcare.

A special statewide task force known as CARS, or Cash Assistance Replacement System, identified and mapped available transportation statewide. As a result of the task force's work, SRS has entered into agreements with the state departments of Administration and Corrections to purchase surplus vehicles. The Department of Corrections repairs and updates these vehicles, which SRS provides to TAF clients who need them to get to work.[13] This is a critical activity in view of the rural nature of most of the state and the dearth of established public transportation. CARS has also been instrumental in pursuing grant opportunities for publicly funded transportation systems for low-income residents of Topeka and Wichita. Other attempts to provide such support include $25-per-month transportation subsidies (or more, if demonstrable need exists), and the client grants for auto purchase and/or repair and maintenance.

Several LAOs are engaged in individual transportation efforts. For example, Kansas City has established a JobLinks transportation pilot program in collaboration with the local transportation authority, which provides bus transportation for TAF clients to selected area employers. Yet despite these efforts, SRS and the LAOs continue to view transportation as a major employment barrier for many TAF clients.

With regard to childcare, SRS has recently authorized higher payments to providers of childcare for TAF recipients engaged in work activities. Families with incomes up to 185 percent of the federal poverty level also receive subsidies for 12 months of childcare after TAF cash benefits end. SRS is also allocating more resources for training childcare providers to enhance the quality of care. Virtually all areas of the state now have an adequate supply of childcare providers, but SRS plans to continue to invest in programs designed to both improve childcare quality and maintain adequate numbers of providers.

In April 1998, SRS doubled allocations for miscellaneous employment support services, such as purchase of cars, uniforms, tools, eyeglasses, cosmetic dental work, and work clothing, to $5,000 per recipient (Kansas SRS 1998b).

Pregnancy Prevention

In an effort to prevent state residents from needing welfare, SRS created the STOP Task Force (Statutory Rape, Teen Pregnancy, and

Out of Wedlock Births Prevention) with representatives from the state departments of Health and Environment, Education, and Corrections, as well as the attorney general's office. The task force issued recommendations in September 1997. (Welfare administrators are highly skeptical that they will ever qualify for the federal bonus available to states that rank in the top five in reducing teen/out-of-wedlock pregnancies.) SRS is likely to proceed very cautiously with the task force recommendations, which may be subject to heightened legislative scrutiny because of their social nature. However, it is fair to speculate that pregnancy prevention efforts will involve extensive agreements with non-profit organizations throughout the state.

Welfare to Work

SRS has worked closely with the state's Department of Human Resources (KDHR) to implement and refine the new Welfare to Work (WTW) program. Federal WTW funds flow directly to KDHR, and then to regional Private Industry Councils (PICs). These councils are responsible for developing and executing local programs designed to enhance the employability of long-term TANF recipients and those facing substantial barriers to employment, including disabled recipients. WTW also serves non-custodial parents responsible for child-support payments for children in TAF cases, with SRS child-support enforcement workers referring non-custodial parents to local WTW offices.

In anticipation of program efforts to maximize employment success among its chronic, long-term welfare recipients, SRS profiled the characteristics of Kansas TAF recipients. The preliminary results suggest that although 60 percent of work-eligible TAF recipients (those not exempt from work requirements) have completed high school or have high school diplomas, 30 percent have learning disabilities and an additional 26 percent have IQ scores below 80.

WTW success will require a close working relationship between SRS and KDHR, both at the state level, where past working relationships have been somewhat contentious, and at the regional office (LAO) level, where working relationships vary.

Implementation Strategies

Administrators have adopted three identifiable strategies to foster implementation of the state's new welfare reforms. These strategies include a variation on Nathan's "second-order devolution" concept (Nathan 1997a), links with other agencies to design specific components of the new welfare program, and a more integrated approach to front-line management of welfare cases.[14]

Decentralization

The administration of welfare services has been centralized in Kansas since the elimination of county responsibility in the 1970s, but SRS has recently given LAO directors greater responsibility for administration and decision making. This strategy has entailed establishing a policy committee composed of the secretary, the deputy secretary, the head of each of the agency's commissions, and the LAO directors.[15] LAO directors influence agency decisions through the committee, and frequently initiate policy refinements and reforms. They also pursue pilot programs and use the committee to share outcomes and seek advice on how to improve specific programs. Most importantly, LAO directors have been granted more latitude to adapt their regional management systems, and to establish relatively informal provider agreements unique to their own region. This decentralization strategy is less drastic than the second-order devolution efforts observed in other states (Nathan 1997a), but both central office and LAO staff say it is critical to welfare reform in Kansas.

The state's decentralization strategy is further strengthened by its willingness to provide local resources. The SRS central office may be inadequately staffed, but administrators have emphasized that they will not reduce LAO staff, and that services to support the work-first objective such as enhanced childcare and transportation support will be generously funded. As of fiscal year 2000, LAOs will be eligible to budget their funds through a block grant designed to increase LAO flexibility. Policymakers clearly expect the LAOs to make generous use of these resources and their newly enhanced autonomy to facilitate the objectives of TAF.

SRS use of provider agreements with locally based nonprofits and governmental organizations is consistent with gubernatorial and legislative pressure to restrict the growth of central office staff. Although resources devoted to central office staff are heavily scrutinized (especially by the legislature), resources appear to be readily available for provider agreements and contracts. This type of activity meets the governor's privatization objectives while maintaining the ability of the governor to limit legislative criticism of the "bloated" SRS bureaucracy.[16]

Interagency Links

The welfare administration has created interagency efforts designed primarily to tackle specific TANF recipient needs that cannot be met exclusively by SRS services. Several of these efforts have attracted the interest of other states.

One such link provides mandatory substance abuse screening for TANF recipients and referral to regional substance abuse centers for additional diagnosis and treatment. Recipients combine treatment, which is required, with a work experience component. SRS has also partnered with the Kansas Coalition against Sexual and Domestic Violence to cross train caseworkers and domestic violence (DV) counselors, to locate DV counselors in larger SRS field offices, and to enable SRS caseworkers to grant good-cause waivers from work requirements for qualified DV victims.

An interagency council has also been established to deal with teen and out-of-wedlock pregnancy.

Integration of Front-Line Staff Functions

Kansas has adopted a new approach for front-line caseworkers that integrates the previously segregated functions of income maintenance (IM) and employment preparation services (EPS). The new IM/EPS workers are responsible for determining eligibility, awarding cash and food stamp benefits, and providing employment services through assessment and referral to other service providers.

The SRS central office has also combined IM and EPS functions into one new commission. Although the shift in the central office proceeded relatively smoothly, implementation in the field has been more contentious and stressful, and some staff members have resigned.

Prior to integration, working relationships between IM and EPS workers varied according to the culture of the individual LAO, the IM and EPS chiefs, and the personalities of the workers. Overall, caseworkers perceived the pre-reform system as highly fragmented: IM and EPS workers were often unaware of each other's decisions concerning a common case, for example. State-wide cross training has helped previously separated IM and EPS workers to integrate both functions. The stress of integration seems to be greatest for EPS workers, who must now master the technical details of determining and reviewing clients' eligibility, even though they are oriented toward the social work aspect of case management and are far less interested in such technical tasks. IM workers, on the other hand, seem more inclined to welcome the opportunity to deal with the whole client.

Integration is occurring as caseworkers face the challenges of implementing new federal and state initiatives. Overall, caseworkers face fundamental changes in their tasks and orientations while holding tremendous power over the potential success of the reforms (Meyers and Dillon 1999).

Information Systems

Like most other states, Kansas is wrestling with difficulties surrounding management information systems (MIS) and "informational federalism" (Gais 1998). The integration of income maintenance and employment preparation, along with other elements of the reforms including child-support enforcement, have required adjustments in the state's TANF information systems. Planned upgrades will integrate the principal system that assesses eligibility for food stamps, Medicaid, TANF, and the state's general assistance program with a second system that tracks support services such as client employment plans, employability assessments, child-support payments, and childcare needs and use. Both these systems collect data through direct input from frontline staff as they open, update, and close TANF cases.[17] The state has established a full IM/EPS system integration deadline of FY2000.

A third system is being developed in response to federal child-support requirements under PRWORA. Kansas was recently notified by the U.S. Department of Health and Human Services that it faces a fine of $850,000 because it had not fully implemented this system by October 1, 1998. Nine other states (including Michigan) have been fined for failing to meet this deadline. The challenges posed by the new system are substantial. Once fully functional, this system will likely be the largest data system operated by the state.

One problem that may delay all TANF information system upgrades is the inability of the state and the private sector to find and retain programmers. This problem is affecting all of the state's social welfare programs.

LAOs have relatively little access to the information that the state data systems collect: Field office staff cannot easily obtain customized management reports from the central MIS. And despite the fact that LAO staff electronically report all TANF activity to the SRS central office, LAO directors complain that they have very little management information, and that monthly aggregated program reports generated by the state are virtually useless. For example, each front-line caseworker receives a case report at the end of the month summarizing his or her own case activity, but summary reports for managerial purposes are not available to their supervisors unless they have constructed an in-house MIS, and many LAOs have still not done so. One goal of the planned integrated system is to allow customized, self-extracting case and general-management reports that will facilitate local program administration.

Another notable weakness in the current MIS is the inability of state officials to identify levels of contractual activity throughout the state. Large statewide contracts, such as that for Electronic Benefits Transfer services for TANF and food stamp clients, are subject to oversight, but local agreements remain largely unmonitored. SRS is currently finalizing development of a new information system that will account for all contracts and provider agreements for PRWORA-related family preservation, foster care, and adoption services.

Evaluation Efforts

At this point, no programwide TANF evaluation efforts exist, although several evaluations are under way for selected components. For example, SRS has contracted with Kansas State University for a study designed to survey families who have left TANF, and to develop a profile of families leaving the program. Like other states, Kansas has experienced significant caseload decreases but has been unable to precisely pinpoint the reasons for these decreases. The study, which is now under way, will survey 5 percent of monthly TANF case closures. While some data will be collected from the state's information systems, the crux of the study will consist of phone and personal interviews with heads of households leaving TANF. A major purpose of the study is to better understand why families leave TANF, what services if any they require after leaving, and why they might find it necessary to reapply to the program.

Conclusion

Welfare reform in Kansas entails important changes among both the welfare population and the welfare bureaucracy. However, the absence of gubernatorial policy entrepreneurship has preserved the incremental nature of the state's social welfare policy, and there is little reason to expect that Kansas will engage in bottom-directed competition with other states.

The welfare bureaucracy has played a primary if not dominant role in crafting the state's new policies. Welfare administrators, supported by other executive branch officials, including the governor, have managed to minimize legislative resistance to their objectives. Legislative and bureaucratic leaders are willing to make modest concessions to interest groups, as evidenced by recent relaxations of work requirements for some TANF adults.

Links and cooperative efforts with other agencies, and with advocacy and other interest groups, have strengthened throughout the design and implementation of welfare reform. Local field office directors enjoy new autonomy as well as influence over central office policy. The most challenging adaptations entail major changes by front-line service workers, who must now move from a segmented to a comprehensive approach, with emphasis on employment and independence as opposed to support and maintenance.

Because neither the Kansas governor nor his welfare administrators are inclined to make radical changes, we can expect Kansas welfare reform to continue to develop incrementally. Future efforts are likely to include continued expansion of the TANF population considered appropriate for work activities, with efforts to include disabled people, those with learning disabilities, and victims of domestic violence. The rhetoric associated with these expansions suggests that expensive support services — such as job retention services — will be used to maximize success for these populations. Selected support services, such as transportation, will be enhanced to maximize work participation rates and ongoing independence from reliance on income support.

References

Advisory Commission on Intergovernmental Relations. 1993. *Federal Regulation of State and Local Governments: The Mixed Record of the 1980s.*Washington, D.C.

American Public Welfare Association. 1997. *State by State Welfare Reform Policy Decisions.* Washington D.C.

Conlan, Timothy. 1991. And the Beat Goes On: Intergovernmental Mandates and Preemption in an Era of Deregulation. *Publius, The Journal of Federalism* Summer: 43-58.

Derthick, Martha. 1972. *New Towns In-Town: Why a Federal Program Failed.* Cambridge, MA: Harvard University Press.

Derthick, Martha. 1970. *The Influence of Federal Grants: Public Assistance in Massachusetts.* Cambridge, MA: Harvard University Press.

Gais, Thomas L. 1998. Welfare, Information and the New Federalism. *The Evaluation Exchange* 4, 2: 12-13.

Gais, Thomas L., Donald J. Boyd, and Elizabeth L. Davis. 1997. The Relationship of the Decline in Welfare Cases to the New Welfare

Law: How Will We Know if It Is Working? *Rockefeller Report*, August 1997. Albany, NY: The Nelson A. Rockefeller Institute of Government.

Gueron, Judith, and Edward Pauly. 1991. *From Welfare to Work*. New York: Russell Sage Foundation.

Johnston, Jocelyn M. 1997. The Medicaid Mandates of the 1980s: An Intergovernmental Perspective. *Public Budgeting and Finance* 17, 1: 3-34.

Johnston, Jocelyn M. 1998. Changing State-Local Fiscal Relations and School Finance in Kansas: Pursuing 'Equity.' *State and Local Government Review* 30, 1: 24-39.

Johnston, Jocelyn M., and Kara Lindaman. 1998. Implementing Welfare Reform in Kansas: Moving, but Not Racing. *Publius: The Journal of Federalism* 28, 3: 123-142.

Johnston, Jocelyn M., and William Duncombe. 1998. Balancing Conflicting Policy Objectives: The Case of School Finance Reform. *Public Administration Review* 48, 2: F145-158.

Johnston, Jocelyn M., Raymond Davis, and Michael Fox. 1998. "Medicaid Reform in Kansas: A Cautious Approach." In *Medicaid Reform and the American States*, Mark R. Daniels, ed. Westport, CT: Greenwood Publishing Group.

Johnston, Jocelyn M., and Barbara S. Romzek. 1999. Privatization and Accountability in Social Service Reform: Theories, Complications, and Conflicts. *Public Administration Review* 58, 5 (September/October): 383-399.

Kansas Department of Social and Rehabilitation Services. 1998a. Response to testimony before the Senate Ways and Means Subcommittee on Social Services, presented by Rochelle Chronister, KDSR Secretary, February 18. Topeka, KS.

Kansas Department of Social and Rehabilitation Services. 1998b. Response to Tufts University Center on Hunger and Poverty Study, presented by Rochelle Chronister, KDSR Secretary, February 23.

Kansas Department of Social and Rehabilitation Services. 1998c. Welfare Reform Update, November 10.

Luce, Thomas F., Jr. 1998. Welfare Reform in Minnesota. Paper presented at the Midwest Political Science Association annual meeting, April 23-25. Chicago.

Lurie, Irene. 1997. Temporary Assistance for Needy Families: A Green Light for the States. *Publius: The Journal of Federalism* 27, 2: 73-89.

Lurie, Irene. 1996. A Lesson From the JOBS Program: Reforming Welfare Must Be Both Dazzling and Dull. *Journal of Policy Analysis and Management* 15, 4: 572-586.

McLean, Jim. 1997. Clinton Hails Cessna Program. *Topeka Capital-Journal*, November 18th.

Mead, Lawrence M. 1996. Welfare Policy: The Administrative Frontier. *Journal of Policy Analysis and Management* 15, 4: 587-600.

Meyers, Marcia K., and Nara Dillon. 1999. "Institutional Paradoxes: Why Welfare Workers Can't Reform Welfare." In *Public Management Reform and Innovation: Research, Theory and Application*, H. George Frederickson and Jocelyn M. Johnston, eds. Tuscaloosa, AL: University of Alabama Press.

Myers, Roger. 1997. SRS Is Losing Its 'Monster' Image. *Topeka Capital-Journal*, July 23.

Nathan, Richard P. 1997a. The Newest New Federalism for Welfare: Where Are We Now and Where Are We Headed? *Rockefeller Report*, October 30. Albany, NY: The Nelson A. Rockefeller Institute of Government.

Nathan, Richard P. 1997b. States and Welfare Reform: Big Change or No Change? *State Fiscal Insights* 1,1. Albany, NY: The Center for the Study of the States, Nelson A. Rockefeller Institute of Government.

Nathan, Richard P., and Thomas L. Gais. 1998. Ten Early Findings About the Newest New Federalism for Welfare. Paper presented at the Woodrow Wilson International Center for Scholars, March 27. Washington, D.C.

Riccio, James, Daniel Friedlander, and Stephen Freedman. 1994. *GAIN: Benefits, Costs, and Three-Year Impacts of a Welfare-to-Work Program.* New York: Manpower Demonstration Research Corp.

Romzek, Barbara S., and Jocelyn M. Johnston. 1999. Reforming Medicaid through Contracting: The Nexus of Implementation and Organizational Culture. *Journal of Public Administration Research and Theory* 9, 1: 107-140.

Schram, Sanford F., Lawrence Nitz, and Gary Krueger. 1998. Without Cause or Effect: Reconsidering Welfare Migration as a Policy Problem. *American Journal of Political Science* 42, 1: 210-30.

Schram, Sanford F., and Carol S. Weissert. 1997. The State of American Federalism, 1996-1997. *Publius: The Journal of Federalism* 27, 2: 1-32.

Sparer, Michael S., and Lawrence D. Brown. 1996. "States and the Health Care Crisis: The Limits and Lessons of Laboratory Federalism." In *Health Policy, Federalism and the American States*, Robert F. Rich and William D. White, eds. Washington, D.C.: The Urban Institute Press.

State of Kansas, Legislative Division of Post Audit. 1995. *Performance Audit Report: Examining Contract Oversight by the Department of Social and Rehabilitation Services.* Topeka, KS.

Tufts University, Center on Hunger and Poverty. 1998. *Are States Improving the Lives of Poor Families? A Scale Measure of State Welfare Policies.* February. Medford, MA.

U.S. Congressional Research Service. 1993. *Medicaid Source Book: Background Data and Analysis, A 1993 Update.* Washington, D.C.: U.S. Government Printing Office.

U.S. Department of Health and Human Services. 1998. *Temporary Assistance for Needy Families (TANF) Program: First Annual Report to Congress*, August.

U.S. General Accounting Office. 1991. *Medicaid Expansions: Coverage Improves but State Fiscal Problems Jeopardize Continued Progress,* June. GAO/HRD — 91-78.

Vobejda, Barbara, and Judith Havemann. 1998. States' Welfare Shift: Stop It Before It Starts, *Washington Post*, August 12.

Walters, Jonathan. 1997. Busting the Welfare Bureaucracy. *Governing* March: 19-23.

Weissert, Carol S. 1998. Welfare Reform in Michigan: Beyond the Headline and the Hype. Paper presented at the annual meeting of the Midwest Political Science Association, April 23-25. Chicago.

Wiseman, Michael. 1996. State Strategies for Welfare Reform: The Wisconsin Story. *Journal of Policy Analysis and Management* 15, 4: 515-46.

Endnotes

1   Kansas' relative position in a continuum of state welfare generosity may not change as a result of the reforms. However, as Sanford Schram has pointed out, one can argue that *all* states have moved closer to the bottom (i.e., most states have made their programs less accessible to the poor).

2   For example, Tufts concluded that Kansas does not exempt parents of children under age one from work requirements, when in fact such parents are exempt.

3   For example, in 1992, Kansas ranked 20th in terms of AFDC family payments, 19th with regard to maximum benefit levels for a family of three, 28th in terms of the household income levels at which AFDC cutoff occurs, and 22nd with regard to AFDC eligibility levels as a percentage of federal poverty levels. In addition, it ranked 23rd in poverty-level coverage for pregnant women under Medicaid expansions, and 30th with regard to eligibility levels for the Medicaid medically needy programs (U.S. Congressional Research Service, 1993). Other interstate analyses rank Kansas among middle states with regard to the comprehensiveness of their Medicaid programs (U.S. GAO, 1991; Johnston, 1997). (These rankings typically assign low rankings — i.e., a rank of 1 — to the most generous social welfare states.)

4   As observed by Sparer and Brown (1996), states may learn from other state policies but they typically craft their own, unique approach. The Sparer and Brown observations are consistent with the Kansas policy. Although Kansas officials learned from the policies of other states (especially Utah and Oregon), the Kansas program reflects to the state's unique conditions.

5   There are exceptions. In response to explicit design requirements imposed by the courts, Kansas has adopted one of the most radical school financing systems in the nation. The system imposes a mandatory, uniform school tax levy on all school districts, as well as a mandatory, uniform per pupil spending level. See Johnston (1998), and Johnston and Duncombe (1998). Kansas was also the first state to privatize foster care and adoption services. The state has espoused an ambitious privatization plan for many of the state's social services, and it may be well ahead of other states on this issue. These privatization initiatives may represent the price that political moderates are willing to pay to avoid serious reductions in social welfare initiatives.

6   The subject of the suit is the alleged federal violation of the Tenth Amendment. The case is currently pending in federal court. At this point, both sides seem committed to taking the case to the U.S. Supreme Court, if necessary. To date, only Utah has opted to disregard federal child support enforcement requirements, thereby forfeiting federal funds. While the federal requirement is not a true regulation, it in effect imposes harsh pen-

alties on states that do not comply with child support enforcement provisions of PRWORA. PRWORA prohibits federal regulation of state activity (Schram and Weissert, 1997; Lurie, 1997), but the incentives for the states to comply with the child support enforcement requirements suggest that in reality, the "grant conditions" is a "mandate" (ACIR 1993; Conlan, 1991; Johnston, 1997).

7   This legislation, HB 2929, enacted provisions similar to those found in other state waivers. It limited GED training to 9 months, instituted family caps (since eliminated), and declared AFDC recipients who had been receiving benefits for 36 months ineligible for additional benefits for a subsequent 3-year period. The provisions proposed by the legislature were originally even more punitive and harsh than those that made their way into law. Despite the efforts of SRS, more moderate legislative factions, and the governor, HB 2929 did not fully protect the original SRS waiver design.

8   Forums were coordinated in part by the Directors of SRS local area offices (LAOs). In general, forums included representatives of food banks, homeless shelters, childrens' advocacy groups, schools, local city/county officials, United Way, local health departments, extension offices, and others. Each LAO produced a unique list of groups invited to participate in the local forum. For the most part, these groups had been involved in prior policy discussions. There is a sense, however, that attention to interest groups was more formal and extensive during the policy formulation stages surrounding the waiver (and consequent TANF-related changes) than in prior policy discussions.

9   Representatives of the following groups also serve on the council: county governments, organized labor, local school districts, the state's League of Municipalities, the financial community, the state's Board of Regents, the state's Department of Administration, and the directors of all SRS field offices.

10 This committee was created during the 1996 session to oversee various changes in SRS programs, including the controversial closure of two state hospitals. The committee's focus on welfare reform is one part of its efforts to monitor the agency and its administrative and programmatic initiatives.

11 The mandatory job search component was based in part on SRS review of similar waiver components in Idaho and Utah.

12 Since the full-family sanction policy was adopted, one-third of sanctioned cases usually comply immediately, and full benefits are restored at once. Of the families who remain sanctioned, nearly 25 percent comply with work requirements within a few months, thereby reopening their cases. Of greater concern are the statistics indicating that roughly half of the initially sanctioned families never comply and ultimately lose full benefits. Because its data systems do not provide information on household well-being

upon termination of TANF, SRS has attempted to ascertain the effects of sanctions by reviewing food bank data and requests for services from other state agencies, including its own Child and Family Services Commission. Administrators have concluded that most sanctioned families are finding alternative sources of support that do not require reliance on these services.

13 The car purchase strategy has generated some challenges, including costs that are higher than anticipated. Some of the challenges are purely logistical. For example, residents from throughout the state must be brought to Topeka (the state capitol) to register and physically take possession of the vehicles.

14 Nathan's concept of second-order devolution refers to state efforts to devolve new welfare responsibilities to local offices of state governments, local governments, and locally based nonprofit and private organizations.

15 SRS commissions include: Income Maintenance/Employment Preparation Services; Children and Family Services; Adult and Medical Services (which administers Medicaid), Alcohol and Drug Abuse Services; Mental Health/Developmental Disabilities Services; Rehabilitation Services; and Administrative Services. Each LAO is staffed by a director, by chiefs responsible for each of the commission functions, and by program staff.

16 Legislative scrutiny stems in part from repeated requests from SRS over the years for supplemental appropriations, required primarily for Medicaid cost overruns in the late 1980s and early 1990s. To quote one Medicaid official, "We can get any resources we want for contracting, but we can't hire central office staff."

17 Under the present system, the Kansas TANF MIS does not track client employment histories or salary information. However, the Department of Human Resources (KDHR) MIS does collect this information, and SRS employees are able to tap into the KDHR systems.

Chapter 4

WISCONSIN'S W-2 PROGRAM: WELFARE AS WE MIGHT COME TO KNOW IT?

Thomas Kaplan

Wisconsin's welfare reform program, Wisconsin Works (W-2), is among the most aggressive of efforts to "end welfare as we know it" and replace it with cash assistance available only through work or work-like activities. The planners of W-2 emphasized seven basic principles:

- ❖ Parents without a disability should work and retain no entitlement to cash assistance in the absence of work.
- ❖ Expectations for success in the labor market should be high; custodial parents will live up or down to the expectations imposed upon them.
- ❖ All cash benefits should be time-limited.
- ❖ Government programs should provide childcare and health care assistance to the working poor, defined as families with incomes up to 200 percent of the federal poverty line, not just to public assistance recipients. (W-2 grants and employment assistance are available only to families with incomes below 115 percent of the poverty line.)

❖ Those who receive grants and other benefits should face the conditions that affect the working poor: recipients should have to work; their first grant check should come only after a period of work; grant levels should not vary by family size; workers who receive public childcare assistance should have to pay part of the cost of their benefits; and program participants should receive all child support paid on behalf of their resident children.

❖ The administration of public assistance should be determined by competition to meet selected outcomes. Key administrative choices ought not rest upon traditional relations between the state and its counties, or traditional conceptions that only public employees should have access to sensitive information and control benefits.

❖ Direct-service staff should offer program participants only as much as the participants ask for or need: "Many persons will do much better with just a light touch" (Wisconsin Department of Workforce Development 1997b, I-1).

W-2 designers have tried to put their principles into operation through several components. Participation requirements for low-income parents begin when the youngest child is 12 weeks old. The parents are assigned to a financial and employment planner (FEP), who places them on one of four steps of a "self-sufficiency ladder" and helps and encourages them to move up the ladder to greater independence, as indicated by the four levels in Table 1. Two-parent families are eligible for all W-2 services if the families meet income and asset restrictions, although some services are restricted to the parent deemed the primary earner. W-2 recipients in the two lower tiers technically receive a monthly grant, which drops by $5.15 for each hour of failure to participate without good cause.

Unlike the AFDC program, the amount of W-2 assistance depends not on family size but on the case head's hours of participation and level on the W-2 self-sufficiency ladder. Participation in the overall program is limited to five years, the maximum period for which the federal government will support most recipients under Temporary Assistance for Needy Families (TANF). Each level on the self-sufficiency ladder also has time limits, with extensions possible on a case-by-case basis.

Table 1
Levels and Key Provisions of W-2

Level of W-2	Basic Income Package	Time Required of Recipients	Program Time Limits	Childcare Co-payment ($/mo)	
				Licensed Care	Certified Care
Unsubsidized employment	Market wage + food employment stamps + Earned Income Tax Credit (EITC)	40 hr/wk standard	None	$101–$134	$71–$92
Trial job (W-2 pays maximum of $300/mo to employer)	At least minimum wage + food stamps + EITC	40 hr/wk standard	Per job: 3 mo, with an option for one 3-mo extension; total: 24 mo	$55	$38
Community service job	$673/mo + food stamps (no EITC)	30 hr/wk standard, and up to 10 hr/wk in education and training	Per job: 6 mo, with an option for one 3-mo extension; total: 24 mo	$38	$25
W-2 transition	$628/mo + food stamps (no EITC)	28 hr/wk work activities standard, and up to 12 hr/wk education and training	24-mo limit, but extensions permitted on a case-by-case basis	$38	$25

Notes: Estimated childcare co-payments are for a three-person family with two children in childcare and receiving no child-support payment. Trial jobs are assumed to pay minimum wage ($5.15 per hour, or $858 per month), and pay for unsubsidized employment is assumed to range from $6 to $7 per hour, or $1,000 to $1,170 per month. Licensed childcare providers must meet higher standards than those who are certified.

Sources: Folk (1996) and presentation materials created by the Wisconsin Department of Workforce Development.

W-2 eliminates the previous practice under which child-support income beyond the first $50 each month goes to public agencies to reimburse welfare expenditures, so most W-2 participants keep all child support paid on their behalf. The program has from its inception also offered significant assistance with childcare. The childcare benefit requires a participant co-payment, based on family income and the number of children in care. The co-payments do not exceed 16 percent of family income and are 30 percent lower for childcare certified by a county rather than fully licensed by the state. Wisconsin has also received approval of a federal waiver to expand the current Medicaid program to serve most W-2 participants as well as families with incomes up to 200 percent of the federal poverty line. Under the waiver, which became effective on July 1, 1999, the state offers a new form of insurance, called BadgerCare, that extends the state's current Medicaid benefits to a broader population, including all W-2 participants who do not have employer-paid insurance. Families with incomes above 150 percent of the poverty line pay a monthly premium of three percent of family income.

In most Wisconsin counties, AFDC income maintenance workers have become FEPs, with broader responsibilities for determining W-2 tier placement, encouraging movement toward greater independence, and making judgments about whether and when to sanction program participants. But the situation is quite different in Milwaukee County, which during the W-2 planning period contained 60 percent of the AFDC recipients and, since the start of W-2 in September 1997, has included more than 80 percent of W-2 participants in the state. Using a proposal developed by researchers at the University of Wisconsin-Milwaukee, the state divided the county into six regions, each of which included some portion of the Milwaukee central city. The state then allowed any agency — private for-profit, private not-for-profit, or public — to bid to become the W-2 provider in that region. Five private agencies were selected, with one agency covering two regions.

Private agencies also operate W-2 in 8 of Wisconsin's other 71 counties. The private contractual arrangements in Milwaukee and elsewhere emerged with only muted controversy because many county AFDC agencies obtained a "right of first selection," which exempted them from having to compete for the W-2 contract during both the initial contract period (September 1997-December 1999) and a second contract period (January 2000-December 2001). Counties received a right of first selection in the initial contract if they had met thresholds of AFDC case reductions and participant engagement. Public and private agencies already operating W-2 could receive a right of first selection for the subsequent contract based on their ratio of staff to participants, percentage of cases meeting full-activity requirements, percentage with an employability plan, percentage that returned to a W-2 grant after a job placement, and several "best practice" criteria, including the pursuit of high school equivalency degrees and the development of contractual arrangements with faith-based organizations. A total of 62 of the 75 agencies administering W-2, including all 5 of the Milwaukee agencies, received a right of first selection for the 2000-2001 contract.

In a state economy characterized by low rates of unemployment, the W-2 program assumes that the obligation for finding a job rests primarily with the W-2 participant. Many FEPs counsel participants on finding employment settings where they might be most likely to attain a job and on maximizing their attractiveness to such employers. The FEPs may also enroll participants in job clubs and provide case management, which, at its most intensive, could involve frequent discussion, advice, and review of both successful and unsuccessful job interviews.

Many W-2 agencies place a heavy rhetorical emphasis on the five-year limit on cash benefits, stressing in sessions with participants that the economy is good, that most people can find an unsubsidized job, and that anyone who can obtain an unsubsidized job should do so immediately because, if the economy deteriorates, they may have a future need for cash assistance.[1]

Sanctions in W-2 occur for two reasons; the most likely is missed hours of assignment in a W-2 transition or community service slot. If this occurs, the FEP determines if a valid reason existed, and can reduce the monthly grant by $5.15 for each missed hour. Sanctions can also arise from failure of school-age children to attend school (although not until after at least two attempts by the FEP to meet with the family to determine any barriers to school attendance and develop strategies to overcome them). The use of sanctions has not yet been a controversial element of W-2, although as this chapter notes, below, sanctions for missed hours have come to affect a significant portion of the caseload.

Local W-2 agencies may use their general resources for transportation support, and the state also makes available $2 million annually for special transportation projects to assist W-2 participants. The state's W-2 policy document requires agencies to plan for the general transportation needs of their W-2 clientele, and to promote options such as employer van pools, special loan programs for automobile purchases through local financial institutions, and volunteer driver programs (Wisconsin Department of Workforce Development 1997b, pp. IV-15-17). Moreover, most W-2 agencies routinely provide free passes to W-2 participants with access to urban bus systems. As is generally true of W-2, however, final responsibility for overcoming transportation barriers lies with the participant, not the agency.

As required under TANF, the Wisconsin W-2 program requires teen parents to attend high school and live in an adult-supervised setting. Unless a county child welfare agency has made a formal finding that the minor parent has been abused or neglected or is in danger of abuse or neglect, the minor parent must live with a parent or other relative.

Wisconsin Governor Tommy Thompson has stressed repeatedly that W-2 is a model for other states. "Ours was the first welfare-to-work program in the nation," he said in a 1998 press release (Office of the Wisconsin Governor), "and it remains a model for other states to follow." Five key features of W-2, each with important implications that are still unfolding, appear to be at least unusual and perhaps unique.

Distinctive Features of Wisconsin Works

The Promptness of Financial Penalties

One atypical feature is the lack of a grace period for participants and quick application of financial penalties. New applicants to W-2 see a financial and employment planner within five working days after they confirm their intention to apply and — if their income, assets, residency, custody of children, and Social Security number can be verified in time — must be assigned to a W-2 placement within seven working days after that. Failure to participate as assigned can result in immediate financial penalties.

The top rung of the W-2 ladder requires a participant to find an unsubsidized job. The state's W-2 policy document notes that "while W-2 agencies must provide sufficient subsidized employment opportunities to eligible individuals, there is no entitlement to cash payments. Placement in a subsidized position is appropriate only for individuals with barriers to unsubsidized employment, as determined by the W-2 agency." Participants may receive job-access loans from their W-2 agencies, if the loans are deemed necessary to obtain or continue employment, and if repayment within a year appears likely. But no cash grant is available during the job search process or in the initial weeks of employment before the first paycheck, or if the participant does not succeed in finding a job. (In many W-2 agencies, however, standard practice is to limit the period of initial job search to seven to ten days before giving strong consideration to placement in a lower level of W-2.)

Participants judged unsuitable for a regular unsubsidized job may be placed in a trial job, in which participants receive income from an employer whose costs are partially reimbursed by the W-2 agency. Participants in this W-2 rung who fail to show up for work are not paid. For the two lower levels of W-2, the penalty of $5.15 is applied for each missed hour of participation without good cause. Full participants in a community service job, for example, receive $673 per month, but the hourly penalty of $5.15 would reduce that grant to zero after 131 hours (slightly over three weeks) of unexcused nonparticipation in a month.[2] The participant could also receive a "strike" for patterns of nonparticipation or failure to cooperate. Participants who receive three strikes at one level of W-2 lose all further eligibility for services in that level (Wisconsin Department of Workforce Development 1997b, p. II-69).

Other states also impose immediate obligations on their TANF participants. The Web site of the National Governors' Association (www.nga.org) indicates that 11 states, including Wisconsin, require immediate work, but some states allow clients to satisfy these requirements by signing a contract requiring movement toward work or attending orientation or job search sessions. In Wisconsin, the FEP has immediate authority to determine a placement, although the FEP is required to develop an employability plan and to attempt to secure the participant's signature on it, and no grace period is available before financial sanctions apply.

Minimal Emphasis on Social Contracts

A second unusual feature of W-2 is its minimal emphasis on social contract language in which the state and the public assistance recipient agree on reciprocal obligations — the one side to make opportunities available and the other to pursue those opportunities. The primary focus of W-2 is on the participant's obligations to follow the employability plan or, if considered ready for an unsubsidized job, to secure one. The emphasis is not on the responsibilities of the state or the W-2 agency to find jobs for participants or to train them for emerging opportunities. The difference between Wisconsin and some other states in this regard is subtle but meaningful. W-2 provides help to program participants with childcare and health care, and FEPs can excuse participants from work requirements if childcare is unavailable. Moreover, the administrative rules for W-2 require local agencies "in consultation with the W-2 participant [to] develop a written employability plan for a W-2 participant which includes the participant's W-2 employment position placement, required activities . . . and an identified unsubsidized employment goal" (Wisconsin Department of Workforce Development 1997a, 17). But unlike many states, the FEP has complete discretion to determine if childcare is unavailable and full authority to determine whether a participant needs a subsidized job. An applicant can appeal a decision of the FEP to the W-2 agency, which must rule on the FEP's decision within 45 days, but even if the appeal is successful, the applicant receives no back payment for the appeal period (Wisconsin Department of Workforce Development 1997b, p. IV-18).

The Centrality of Work

More than many states, Wisconsin has taken pains to emphasize the centrality of work from the first contact of participants with the public assistance system. In every Wisconsin county, potential participants in W-2 or the food stamp program go to job centers, not welfare offices. Most job centers also serve workers who are not welfare participants, providing general labor exchange services, basic training for job seekers, and short-term childcare services for "customers." The work motif is similarly apparent in the structure of assistance programs, which are designed to require beneficiaries to face conditions affecting low-wage workers generally: the first W-2 grant check comes only after a period of work and does not vary with family size; those who receive public childcare assistance must pay part of the cost of their benefits; and program participants receive all child support paid on behalf of their resident children.

Pass-Through of Child-Support Benefits

Wisconsin is the only state that has chosen to pass through all child support to custodial parents (with the exception of up to 4,000 families in a control group who receive partial payments to facilitate program evaluation). In fact, 30 states plus the District of Columbia have used their new flexibility under TANF to move in the opposite direction, keeping for the government all child support paid on behalf of a TANF family (U.S. Department of Health and Human Services 1997). Wisconsin's policy marks a change from AFDC, when a family could keep only $50 per month of child support paid on the family's behalf; any additional payments reimbursed the state and federal governments for their AFDC expenditures.

The Use of Private Agencies

In most of Wisconsin's 72 counties, the agency operating W-2 is the same agency that operated AFDC, the county social or human services department. However, in 9 counties, private agencies operate W-2 under a contract with the state. Since one of those 9 counties is Milwaukee, which enrolled over 80 percent of all W-2 participants during the first 18 months of operation, the program is in a sense primarily contracted to private agencies. Private W-2 agencies have the same responsibilities as public W-2 agencies for core services, including determining clients' eligibility for W-2, placing them in one of the four tiers and a particular assignment within a tier, and deciding on financial penalties. Such public-private arrangements are unusual. Under AFDC, private agencies often provided welfare-to-work services, but only public agencies could have access to the income and asset information used to determine eligibility and benefits, and only public employees controlled program benefits. Even under TANF, according to a spokesperson for the U.S. Department of Health and Human Services, "nowhere else has a state delegated the administration of welfare to agencies other than governments" (Huston 1998c).

The Policy Origins of W-2

In a state that at the start of Republican Governor Tommy Thompson's administration in 1986 offered the fifth-highest AFDC benefit levels in the country (U.S. House of Representatives 1992), the transition to a program with the unusual features of W-2 calls for some explanation. The AFDC waivers that preceded W-2 are more fully described elsewhere (Corbett 1995; Wiseman 1996); this section briefly reviews the early policy modifications before exploring more recent changes.

The beginnings of W-2 extend at least to the 1986 gubernatorial election in Wisconsin, when Thompson, then minority leader of the State Assembly, was elected governor against a one-term Democratic incumbent. Many factors contributed to Thompson's victory, including unpopular tax increases proposed and implemented by the incumbent governor, a controversial effort to place a new prison near downtown Milwaukee, and Thompson's sheer hard work during the campaign. Welfare issues also played a role. The incumbent governor, who had begun ambitious changes in child-support policy, and employment and training reforms similar to those required by subsequent federal JOBS legislation,[3] chose, for reasons still unclear, not to discuss these innovations during his re-election campaign. Thompson, on the other hand, emphasized the state's high AFDC benefit levels, and argued that some people were moving to Wisconsin to take advantage of the generous benefits. A central feature of his campaign was a promise to reduce AFDC benefits and stop welfare-induced migration to the state.

After his election, Governor Thompson moved quickly to reduce AFDC benefits by 6 percent and make welfare reform a prominent theme of his administration. He did so primarily through use of the liberalized federal waiver policy that permitted deviation from AFDC rules and that became available during the mid-1980s. The Thompson administration made three sets of waiver proposals. The first, in the late 1980s, centered on Learnfare, one of the earliest attempts to condition full AFDC benefits on behavior — in this case, on school attendance by teens. The second group of waivers was implemented in 1992 when Governor Thompson enjoyed a close friendship with President George Bush, who was encouraging states to try bolder welfare reforms. The most notable initiatives here included the Two-Tier Benefit proposal, which gave AFDC recipients new to Wisconsin up to six months of assistance at the benefit level they would have received in their old state, and the Parental and Family Responsibility (PFR) initiative. PFR, dubbed Bridefare by its opponents, was an attempt to modify fertility and family-formation behavior among teens and improve their economic well-being by granting young cohabiting couples liberalized access to AFDC in return for reduced grant increases for second children and increased work obligations for fathers. The third set of waiver proposals centered on a two-county (Fond du Lac and Pierce) demonstration program called Work Not Welfare (WNW), which introduced strict work requirements and a two-year time limit on benefits and sought to change the mission of welfare offices.

In hindsight, it is tempting to view these programs as orderly steps on the road to W-2, but the central themes of the new program — personal responsibility, work, and revamping the mission of welfare offices — emerged only gradually and haltingly from a decade of experimentation. Perhaps no single welfare reform program with the scope of W-2 would have emerged, at least in the pre-TANF period, if Democrats in the Wisconsin legislature had not engaged in a kind of political contest over the WNW proposal.

The Work Not Welfare waiver request was widely viewed, when submitted in July 1993, as the governor's attempt to beat President Bill Clinton to a time-limited welfare system. In response, several Wisconsin Democrats, apparently tired of reacting to (and generally accepting) Governor Thompson's welfare proposals, tried to seize the initiative by claiming that WNW merely tinkered with the welfare system, when it really needed replacement. When WNW came before the state legislature for authorization, the Democrats accepted the proposal but added a requirement, through an amendment proposed by an inner-city Milwaukee legislator, that AFDC must end in Wisconsin, to be replaced by a wholly new system before December 31, 1998.

The amended bill imposed several restrictions on the replacement program, stipulating that it had to assure adequate childcare and health care, guarantee income for those who could not work, and provide jobs for people who could work but were unable to find employment. Using his extensive item veto authority, however, the governor left in the bill language specifying that AFDC must end and that the Wisconsin Department of Health and Social Services (DHSS) must propose a replacement for it by December 1, 1995, but deleted all restrictions on the new program. The governor thus crafted a requirement that a cabinet agency under his direct control propose an indeterminate replacement for a welfare system now mandated to end. As with AFDC under the Social Security Act of 1935, and the War on Poverty under the Economic Opportunity Act of 1964 (Witte 1963; Gillette 1996), the new approach to welfare would be designed, at least in this state, by the executive rather than the legislative branch.

The Politics of Program Design

As soon as the governor signed the bill, the Hudson Institute, a conservative think tank with national influence, offered to open a Wisconsin office and help develop the nation's first post-AFDC policy as a model for the country. The state accepted the offer. Key participants in the development effort were Andrew Bush, a consultant from the Hudson Institute with experience as Republican staff for the U.S. House Ways and Means Committee; Shannon Christian, director of planning for DHSS and a former official in the Bush administration; Laura Kaye, a DHSS planner; Anna Kondratas, then with the Hudson Institute and best known for her book *Out of the Poverty Trap: A Conservative Strategy for Welfare Reform* (Butler and Kondratas 1987); Jean Rogers, the director of state welfare programs and formerly a Republican Party activist in Wisconsin; Jason Turner, employment and training director in DHSS and also a former official in the Bush administration; and Gerald Whitburn, then secretary of DHSS. The Hudson Institute and three foundations, one generally viewed as conservative (the Bradley Foundation) and two as liberal (the Annie E. Casey and Charles Stewart Mott foundations), provided resources to help with planning.

The planning process was not publicized as it occurred — meetings were held in what participants referred to as a secure "war room" — and few details have become available. A key objective was to develop a detailed written plan to which others could react, while avoiding premature exposure that might enable opponents to mobilize resistance before the hopefully dramatic vision of W-2 was deemed ready for broad consumption. The architects of W-2 believed their program would transform the welfare debate, and they did not want to defend a partial vision. The group finished its work in the summer of 1995, and the governor announced the completed

W-2 proposal (Wisconsin Department of Health and Social Services 1995) with some fanfare that August.

Major Policy Issues

With a strong and popular governor making a request that would help define him nationally to a state legislature controlled by members of his own party, ultimate passage of W-2 seemed assured. The bill did in fact pass relatively promptly — it was introduced in October 1995 and passed in March 1996 — but several W-2 issues were intensely discussed and, in some cases, altered during the six months of legislative consideration.

Program administration. The architects of W-2 sought a dramatic change in assistance to poor families, and they believed that public welfare workers and managers might not be able to adapt. The administration thus proposed to identify geographic areas for local administration of W-2 and to allow any agency — public or private, profit or not-for-profit — to bid to operate the program. Several county boards of supervisors, public welfare officials, and public employee unions expressed concern about this approach, and a legislative compromise emerged. All county welfare agencies were subject to a pre-W-2 trial period during which they were evaluated against standards of engagement in program requirements and expected reductions in AFDC caseloads. Counties meeting the standards, as most did, had the right to administer the W-2 program in their county for the initial contract period (September 1997 through December 1999).

Childcare. The governor's initial proposal sought to expand the supply of childcare by creating a less-regulated category: those who provided care to no more than four children in their home could be "provisionally" certified and thereby avoid the 15 hours of training required for full county-level certification. The proposal also sought to expand the use of childcare through higher public payments, while requiring participants to pay a share. Despite controversy, the training change passed largely intact, but Republican legislators took the lead in using funds derived from falling welfare caseloads and an initially generous federal block grant to increase childcare resources substantially and reduce the level of co-payments by recipients.

Health care. The Thompson administration argued that loss of health care benefits under the AFDC system acted as a strong disincentive for people to move into the labor market. The proposed response was to provide a transitional cushion of expanded Medicaid benefits to the working poor. The administration said this would require no new public expenditures, proposing to impose new monthly premiums and restrict benefits to those with no employer-provided insurance. The proposal would have imposed new premiums on existing Medicaid client groups, a change that required a federal Medicaid waiver. Health care provider and advocacy groups in Wisconsin criticized the proposal, and the federal government declined to grant the waiver.

However, federal passage of the Children's Health Insurance Program (CHIP) in the Budget Act of 1997 offered a new opportunity. The Thompson administration crafted a proposal to use new resources from CHIP to offer Medicaid benefits to the full W-2 population without imposing premiums on existing Medicaid-eligible groups. The state developed a revised health care plan, titled BadgerCare, incorporating the new federal resources and offering the state's complete package of Medicaid benefits to any uninsured family with children with income below 200 percent of the federal poverty line. Those between 150 percent and 200 percent of poverty would pay a monthly premium of, at most, 3 percent of income. After much state-federal negotiation concerning the degree to which this plan was a guaranteed entitlement, the parties forged a compromise: the state agreed to assure full services, with no waiting lists, to all those eligible for the program, and the federal government agreed to allow Wisconsin to reduce income-eligibility thresholds if needed to protect the state's budget assumptions. The new program took effect on July 1, 1999.

Grants or wages? The architects of W-2 argued that community service and transition slots — the two lowest rungs of the W-2 ladder — were not real jobs and did not need to pay minimum wage, provide eligibility for state and federal Earned Income Tax Credits, impose payroll tax requirements, or confer Social Security or Unemployment Insurance benefits. In contrast, a coalition led by Milwaukee Mayor John Norquist viewed the positions as real employment for those left behind by a labor market that creates, at least in some parts of the state, too few jobs. Although the mayor and his supporters argued unsuccessfully for broader minimum wage and benefit provisions, they did obtain budget approval for allowing two W-2 agencies in Milwaukee to place community service participants in wage-paying jobs, and for allowing all other W-2 agencies to offer wage-paying community service jobs for up to 15 hours per week. These options became available on February 1, 1999.

Work-first versus human capital development. W-2 was not designed to emphasize preparation for higher-paying jobs that would require extensive training. "Education and training under W-2 should prepare participants for entry-level employment," and "full-time education and training is not acceptable," says the W-2 policy document (Wisconsin Department of Workforce Development 1997b, II-52–53). Participants in W-2 transition and community service job programs can receive 10-12 hours of training per week (more in some weeks if the average is 10-12), but the training must relate directly to jobs immediately obtainable after brief preparation, such as food service and nursing assistant positions. Critics have argued that W-2 should prepare participants for higher-paying jobs that would allow full independence, and in February 1998 the Thompson administration created a W-2 Workforce Training Options task force to discuss this (Flaherty 1998). The five private agencies operating W-2 in Milwaukee County also met with state legislators to propose that selected participants be reimbursed for more training hours (Huston 1998b), but the issue remains under discussion.

Interviews I have held with W-2 agency staff suggest that formal job training appears to be an increasingly frequent assignment, at least in the Milwaukee W-2 agencies. Moreover, state policies have been modified to allow classroom training for more than 10 hours per week if the training occurs at a central community service work site (Wisconsin Department of Workforce Development 1998, p. 6-6). Still, the broad policy of restricting classroom training to a part-time activity of relatively short duration and aimed at preparation for entry-level positions continues.

Understanding the Political Consensus

Despite such policy modifications, the legislature did not change the fundamental characteristics of W-2. Participants must work, and agencies have no obligation to provide extensive educational support for clients or find work for those whom they consider appropriate for unsubsidized employment. The most significant change from the original conception of W-2 concerned the awarding of contracts to W-2 agencies, with most counties obtaining a right of first selection for the initial contract period. Even this provision, however, represented no sharp change from the original conception, as the right of first selection did not affect Milwaukee County.

Not only did the fundamental characteristics of the W-2 proposal remain unchanged, but few people pressed for fundamental changes, and little public debate over the end of an entitlement to income occurred while legislators formulated W-2. The archbishop of the Milwaukee Catholic Archdiocese did argue strongly and publicly that guaranteed social provision for the poor was a moral necessity that W-2 failed to provide. In an op-ed essay published in the *Washington Post* on July 4, 1996, Archbishop Rembert Weakland called W-2 a "tragedy for the poor and a moral blemish on the earth's most affluent society" (quoted in Aukofer 1996). The archbishop urged President Clinton to deny the needed waivers for W-2, a request rendered moot by the enactment of TANF later that summer. The archbishop and the governor (who is Roman Catholic) then engaged in a much-publicized dispute. Governor Thompson said the Bible contains many examples of the need for personal responsibility and for strenuous effort to support one's own family. He said the archbishop, just returned from a six-month sabbatical studying music at Columbia University, "should come back to Wisconsin to read his Bible instead of playing piano in New York" (Jones 1996). The governor also maintained that the "welfare check, which has only served to trap generations in welfare dependency and despair," is the "immoral" force, not W-2 (Dresang 1996). But this flurry occurred four months after passage of W-2, and the archbishop and the governor soon declared a truce.

Some provisions of W-2, especially the full pass-through of child support, received enthusiastic endorsement from all parts of the political spectrum. Liberals approved of the increased income to needy families, and conservatives endorsed the potential for more support from absent fathers. The provision also helped the Thompson administration satisfy its principle of giving recipients of public assistance many of the same obligations and benefits of low-income workers.

The apparent consensus supporting the immediate loss of entitlement, and the shift of obligation to the participant and away from the state, probably derived in part from the strength of the

Wisconsin economy and the ready availability of jobs — although Wisconsin's unemployment rate had been both low and beneath that of the nation during earlier periods when no challenge to the legitimacy of AFDC had emerged.[4]

The explanation also lies in the constraints under which critics of W-2 were forced to operate. A coalition of W-2 opponents formed during legislative consideration of W-2. Members included disability organizations (some parents received AFDC to stay home and care for their disabled children, and some AFDC parents have disabilities), the Welfare Warriors (a group of mothers on public assistance, primarily in Milwaukee), the Wisconsin Council on Children and Families (a long-time statewide advocacy group), the Institute for Wisconsin's Future (generally composed of public and private college faculty and staff), childcare providers and advocates, and the social action committee of the Catholic Archdiocese of Milwaukee. Shortly after Governor Thompson introduced W-2, coalition members decided that, because of broad legislative support for the general direction of W-2, they would not try to defeat the overall initiative, but instead would attempt to change it on its margins. "We've never said that welfare didn't need to be reformed. We've said it had to be done carefully," the director of the Council on Children and Families and a coalition leader later recounted (Dresang 1996).

The coalition did succeed in securing a sizable increase in childcare resources, but the decision to influence W-2 only at the margin also guaranteed political victory for those who wanted to end the entitlement and shift obligations from the state to individuals. Yet the coalition's decision was understandable. Because key members of the Democratic Party, which contained most of the natural allies of the coalition, had already proposed replacing AFDC, opponents' ability to contest W-2 was sharply curtailed. The coalition might have proposed a different kind of replacement, perhaps offering participants a period of assistance without work before withdrawing cash benefits, or making their obligations more directly contingent on the state's provision of services or the availability of jobs. But designing an alternative required more unity than the disparate members of the coalition could achieve.

It is also important to note that some Wisconsin liberals have not just grudgingly accepted W-2. Particularly in Milwaukee, key liberals have enthusiastically endorsed many provisions of the program. One long-time advocate for low-income women, the executive director of the Milwaukee YWCA (a private agency with a state contract to serve W-2 clients), claimed that W-2 "is a tremendous opportunity. It's a once-in-a-lifetime possibility to make families self-sufficient and rebuild the central city" (Stingl 1997). Lawrence Mead (1999) has argued that such liberal acceptance of work-based welfare reform has made Wisconsin unique among (relatively) urban states. Mead suggests that traditions developed under the state's Progressive Party early in the twentieth century endured even after its members moved into the Democratic and Republican parties. The Progressive traditions, now bipartisan, contributed to generally reduced political rancor, a broad acceptance of the centrality of both work and expansive support services, and governmental capacity to carry out complex reform.

Implementing W-2

From 1967 through 1995, all public welfare programs in Wisconsin, including AFDC, had fallen under the purview of the state Department of Health and Social Services (DHSS), which was also responsible for public health, Medicaid, adult and juvenile corrections, child welfare services, and substance abuse and other services. A separate agency, the Department of Industry, Labor, and Human Relations (DILHR), was responsible for unemployment insurance, workers' compensation, workplace safety and health, Job Service labor exchange, and related programs. To emphasize the centrality of work in W-2, the legislation that created the program proposed transferring all public-assistance functions except Medicaid to DILHR, which was then relieved of some building code enforcement responsibilities and renamed the Department of Workforce Development (DWD). The new DWD administers all childcare programs and child support enforcement, along with W-2, food stamps, Supplemental Security Income (SSI), and energy assistance.

Budget Surplus Eases Transition

September 1, 1997, was the first day on which new applicants for public assistance were required to obtain their TANF assistance from W-2 agencies. Because federal regulations require that public employees determine eligibility for food stamps and Medicaid, new applicants for W-2 in Milwaukee and other counties in which the W-2 agency was not the public welfare department had to undergo review and processing by two agencies. To ease this process, Milwaukee County distributed its eligibility and benefits staff among the six W-2 regions. Applicants were thus able to meet with county staff in the same buildings in which they met their FEPs, and most county staff joined small teams with FEPs sharing the same caseload. The collocation and teaming were important innovations, although county economic security staff sometimes did not meet with applicants or process their cases as quickly as either the applicants or W-2 agency staff wished.

AFDC recipients wishing to transfer to W-2 had to come to the W-2 agency and request the transfer. Those who did not respond to letters and, in some cases, phone calls and visits to their homes were dropped from AFDC by March 31, 1998. Not all the conversions from AFDC were to W-2, because Wisconsin had also used its AFDC program to provide assistance to two types of cases in which the adult was not expected to work—namely, families in which the adult was disabled and received SSI (only the children were part of the AFDC grant), and families in which the adult (often a grandparent) was not legally responsible for the children and only the children were part of the AFDC grant. Some 11,000 families in these categories moved to other programs: Caretaker Supplement for those headed by SSI recipients, and Kinship Care for those headed by "nonlegally responsible relatives."

The transition from W-2 to AFDC occurred in the context of a decade-long reduction in the number of AFDC cases in Wisconsin (Figure 1). AFDC caseloads in Wisconsin began a steady decline in 1987, avoided the national increases of the early 1990s, and dropped sharply in the mid-1990s. By 1997, the AFDC caseload had fallen by 80 percent — from over 100,000 cases to about 22,000 cases. As Wisconsin officials developed final plans and budgets for W-2 agencies, AFDC/TANF caseloads continued to fall faster in Wisconsin than anticipated, dropping by 50 percent between December 1996 and December 1997, for example.

A key result was a surplus of resources. The Wisconsin legislature had appropriated funds for the W-2 program, and state administrators had allocated funds to W-2 agencies, based on estimates of much higher caseloads. As a result, W-2 agencies could provide a high level of service to each W-2 participant without worrying

FIGURE 1
AFDC/TANF Caseloads 1987 - 1998

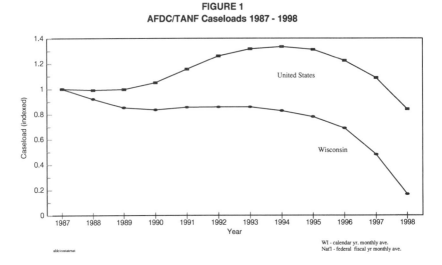

WI - calendar yr. monthly ave.
Nat'l - federal fiscal yr monthly ave.

Notes: Figures include both the AFDC-Basic and AFDC-Unemployed Parent programs. All annual figures are averages of the 12 monthly figures for the year. Both the U.S. and Wisconsin caseload figures are indexed to 1 in 1987 to show comparative trends over the subsequent decade.

Sources: U.S. figures are unpublished data from the Administration for Children and Families, U.S. Department of Health and Human Services. Wisconsin figures are unpublished data from the Research and Statistics Section, Bureau of Welfare Initiatives, Wisconsin Department of Workforce Development.

about cost overruns, cash flow problems, or difficulties in meeting net revenue projections. The unexpected level of financial comfort eased the implementation process in the early months of W-2 and provided context for the following trends in the early stages of W-2.

Informal Limits on Unsubsidized Placements

Because FEPs, rather than the actual labor market experience of participants, determine whether a participant is ready for an unsubsidized job, and because W-2 agencies benefit financially by restricting services to participants, a major concern of W-2 skeptics has been that agencies would too aggressively assign participants to unsubsidized placements, whether or not they were able to find jobs. The participants could then languish in the labor market with no income, their FEPs maintaining that they could find a job if they tried harder or differently. In the first few months of W-2 operation in Milwaukee, the county legal services office heard complaints of just such practices. However, the complaints seem to have declined. With the ample financial resources available for current W-2 participants, the Milwaukee agencies have on their own developed informal limits on the length of time participants can be in the job market without a subsidy. Participants who do not find a job within that time limit receive a community service job while FEPs evaluate the reasons for their lack of success in the labor market.

Heavy Use of Community Service Placements

Especially among the Milwaukee W-2 agencies, placement in a community service job was initially almost a default assignment, representing about 63 percent of all W-2 placements in Milwaukee as of April 30, 1998. This pattern stemmed in part from the requirement for rapid conversion of AFDC participants to W-2. Some W-2 agencies, in their rush to convert AFDC participants before the March 31 deadline, held three or four group sessions per day for 30 to 40 AFDC recipients simultaneously, at which they filled out and signed their employability plans and session leaders instructed them to select community service as their preferred initial assignment. (The agencies seem to have no trouble finding community service jobs, which range from work as aides in childcare centers to janitorial work in housing authorities to industrial packaging in W-2 agency work centers.) Community service placements have since declined slightly as a share of total placements, but still represented over 59 percent of placements in Milwaukee in February 1999.

The heavy use of community service jobs may also reflect a scarcity of alternatives. Less than 1 percent of placements statewide in August 1998 involved trial jobs; employers seem uninterested in utilizing this category, saying in focus groups and other settings that they would rather hire regular employees who appear qualified — and discharge those whose performance is deemed inadequate — than assume the additional paperwork and oversight associated with trial jobs.[5] Assignments to W-2 transition have been more frequent, accounting for 18 percent of placements statewide as of the end of February 1999. But my own limited observations suggest that such placements are used primarily for parents who are caring for a child with severe disabilities, for participants assigned to a Medicaid-funded outpatient mental health or drug-abuse treatment program, and for participants awaiting placement in the federal Supplemental Security Income program.

Strong Emphasis on the Use of Local Job Centers

The state's promotion of integrated local job centers that provide both welfare and labor exchange programs and serve other citizens along with welfare clients predated W-2. A large statewide task force organized in 1985 proposed that the state develop a funding structure that would reward local areas attempting such collocation. A rural area in southwestern Wisconsin was first to try the concept, and Kenosha County in southeastern Wisconsin became the first urban program. Other large (by Wisconsin standards) counties followed. After passage of the federal JOBS legislation in 1988, some county job centers expanded to include the private agencies that provided JOBS programming in many larger counties. Programs for seniors and people with disabilities (including those that determine food stamp eligibility and benefits for these populations) often remained in a separate building, but the most expansive job centers, such as the Kenosha center, incorporated mental health, alcohol and other drug abuse, Head Start, public health, and vocational-technical college offices and services. Services have now become so integrated in many job centers that W-2 clients placed in unsubsidized jobs are indistinguishable from clients of other programs.

New Federal Welfare-to-Work Funds Not Used for W-2

Wisconsin's share of Welfare-to-Work funding from the U.S. Department of Labor for the first year of the program totaled some $13 million. The state elected to retain the maximum amount allowed under federal law (15 percent) for allocation by the state; the remaining 85 percent will go (as required by federal law) to the state's 11 service delivery areas. Of its 15 percent ($1.9 million), the state awarded $1.1 million to the Department of Corrections for job readiness and employment assistance services to probationers, parolees, and minimum security inmates nearing release; $90,000 to a migrant services organization for employment readiness services for families not yet eligible for W-2 because they have not resided in the state for 60 days; $180,000 to agencies serving Southeast Asians, for services such as assistance in obtaining drivers' licenses and employment services for second wage-earning parents; $180,000 to help noncustodial parents enter apprenticeship programs; and $400,000 for state administration, including enhancements to the state computer system to allow reporting of Welfare-to-Work expenditures and services to the federal government.

Most of the federal funds are reserved for the service delivery areas, and federal law gives them much autonomy in determining how to allocate the resources, so long as they go to populations with designated barriers to employment or other characteristics typical of long-term welfare recipients. But Wisconsin has urged local areas to concentrate on services to noncustodial parents, and to avoid funding programs for people who live with children and could receive W-2 employment services. If service delivery areas do provide services for W-2 participants, they are asked to demonstrate that the W-2 agencies have insufficient capacity to provide the services. Nearly 70 percent of the service delivery area funds are projected to go to Milwaukee County. At this writing, the Milwaukee service delivery area has decided to spend $720,000 to help noncustodial parents with criminal records obtain and keep jobs; $660,000 to help Latino fathers not living with their children find jobs and pay child support; $520,000 to Legal Services to provide advice and representation to potential workers whose legal troubles keep them from finding or retaining jobs; and $230,000 for other employment services to noncustodial parents.

Low Initial Use and Administrative Complexity of Childcare Resources

One of the more ambitious aspects of W-2 has been its effort to create a simpler, better-funded, and more efficient system of childcare assistance for families below 200 percent of the federal poverty line. The program has done this by reducing five different childcare programs to one, with one set of benefits and co-payments and no waiting list. In the legislation creating W-2, the state doubled over a period of two years the annual funds available for childcare, increasing them from $90 million in 1996-97 to $180 million in 1998-99 (Wisconsin Legislative Fiscal Bureau 1997).

However, the new resources went largely unused. State budget estimates assumed that 77,000 children would be in state-supported childcare in December 1997. The actual number was 19,500, which was less than the total served or on waiting lists only a year earlier. The general decline in W-2 caseloads may have been partly responsible, although eligibility for childcare assistance is defined by income and is not limited to W-2 employment participants. Lack of publicity and relatively high co-payment requirements may have also played a role. Administrative problems are another reason for the low use of childcare funds, particularly in Milwaukee. W-2 agencies are responsible for assessing eligibility for childcare assistance and discussing co-payment obligations and the availability of potential providers. Social service departments are responsible for certifying providers, setting maximum reimbursement rates equal to the 75th percentile of the local market for most providers (the 50th percentile for providers with only provisional certification), and reimbursing providers.

In most counties, W-2 and county social service agencies are the same, but in Milwaukee, links between W-2 agencies and the county have been strained. Previous audits had faulted the county social service agency for insufficient controls over childcare payments, citing instances in which the agency reimbursed providers for more children than their licensure or certification allowed. Partly in an effort to address such problems, the Milwaukee County agency was slow to reimburse providers of childcare, and some providers refused to continue providing care to some participants' children. "Mothers were getting so tangled in red tape that they were simply giving up," said one state senator (Dresang 1998). In October 1998 the state provided additional funding to Milwaukee County to accelerate the process of paying childcare providers and auditing the expenditures.

The Important Role of FEPs

Several observers have noted the significant role that case managers play in welfare-to-work programs (Bardach 1997; Mead 1997). In W-2, FEPs determine individual employability plans, assign participants to levels of W-2 and particular assignments within each level, suggest appropriate community resources, motivate participants to comply with the letter and spirit of W-2, and sanction them for failure to comply. If the FEPs work for public agencies, they determine eligibility for food stamps and Medicaid. In many W-2 agencies,

FEPs are also responsible for initial sessions with prospective participants, and for diverting them to other programs.

This multiplicity of roles suggests several possible metaphors for what FEPs actually do. An obvious possibility — FEP as social worker — seems to have limited applicability to W-2. As in most states, public agency staff in Wisconsin with degrees and certification in social work generally serve frail seniors, people with disabilities, or families under investigation or receiving services for child abuse and neglect. Wisconsin's FEPs, in contrast, usually have a background as county economic support workers or as staff in a JOBS program, and often do not hold a college degree or professional certification, although some have bachelor's or master's degrees in fields as varied as business administration and vocational rehabilitation.

The much-studied welfare-to-work program of Riverside County, California, suggests another possible metaphor — case manager as salesperson. As part of the interview process to obtain a case manager position, applicants in Riverside County had to simulate selling a used car — suggesting that their role is to sell welfare recipients on the importance, and realistic possibilities, of finding a job. Eugene Bardach (1997) has suggested yet another metaphor—case manager as coach, which seems more descriptive of W-2. Like coaches, Wisconsin FEPs are presumed to have learned their craft more through experience than through college courses or certification programs. Also like coaches, FEPs are presumed to exercise moral authority for the good of their charges. In W-2, much of their claim for moral authority seems to derive from the FEPs' past experience. In every one of the six sessions between FEPs and participants I observed, and in many interviews with FEPs, the FEP has mentioned either her own background as a welfare recipient who achieved independence or her mother's success in moving from economic distress to a more comfortable life.

Evolving Conceptions of Case Management

Jason DeParle of *The New York Times* wrote in 1998 that the customized case management originally envisioned for W-2 has not appeared, at least in Milwaukee County. Rather than carefully guiding participants to greater independence through individualized services, FEPs, according to DeParle (1998), acted more often like harried clerks, sometimes failing even to return the phone calls of participants whose eligibility for childcare funds had inexplicably been denied.

Certainly W-2 planners did not intend that participants should fail to receive childcare benefits to which they were entitled, or that FEPs would fail to return their phone calls.[6] But in its origins, carefully targeted case management was not an unambiguous premise of W-2. Planning documents emphasized "the light touch," under which W-2 "should provide only as much service as an eligible person asks for or needs," as much as they emphasized case management. The introductory section of the W-2 policy document, for example, which describes the "philosophy and goals" of W-2, does not discuss case management at all. W-2 planning documents do include references to case management functions — developing individualized plans for each participant, assessing the effectiveness of the plan, and referring participants as needed to community services. Moreover, the case management aspects of W-2 may have played a more prominent role in the thinking of some local W-2 agencies. However, in the original design of W-2, intensive and carefully calibrated case management received less prominence than has been the case since financial resources sufficient to support considerable case management have become apparent.

Growing Use of Sanctions

Sanctions for missed W-2 transition and community service hours were relatively rare during the first few months of W-2. In the five months between September 1997 and January 1998, 738 sanctions were imposed — an average of some 150 per month, or less than 3 percent of the monthly caseload. Jean Rogers, the chief administrator of W-2, wrote agencies a memo in December 1997 expressing concern that they were failing to promote full engagement among W-2 participants, and urging greater use of sanctions where appropriate (Huston 1998a). The number of sanctions then rose significantly, affecting between 26 percent and 29 percent of all cases in community service and transition assignments in July, August, and September 1998.[7] In March 1999, W-2 agencies sanctioned 42 percent of community service and transition participants. The average penalty in that month was $372 (55 percent of the grant) for community service participants and $212 (34 percent of the grant) for those in W-2 transition.

The rapid increase in sanctions, while reflecting a bold willingness to confront participants who failed to meet W-2 standards, may also indicate flaws in the program's governance. Lawrence Mead, a key influence during the planning of W-2 and a continuing advisor, argued in earlier studies that the best welfare-to-work programs achieved their results with limited use of sanctions. In a study of the Work Incentive (WIN) welfare-to-work programs of the late 1970s, Mead reported that formal sanctions "for noncooperation proved to be weakly or negatively linked to performance, even though they might seem to embody WIN's authority. Overall, the more registrants an office proceeded against in this formal way, the *worse* it performed" (1986, p. 160). Mead noted that one explanation for this paradox was probably a series of court decisions undercutting the authority of WIN offices to enforce sanctions, but he also said that interviews with WIN staff made clear "that the best way to convey obligations was *informally*, earlier in the administrative process. If clients realized when they first entered WIN that the work obligation was serious, they rarely needed discipline later." Mead continued this theme in a later work, arguing that while effective programs "do penalize people who refuse to cooperate, they prefer to exert authority more informally. They give direction through a process of intense interaction with the clients that involves give and take. Relationships grow up among the clients as well as between them and the staff, and these ties become the real means of motivating work effort, transcending the more formal authority that initially brings people into the program" (1992, pp. 175-176).

W-2 is still in its early stages of development, and program managers may have some basis for arguing that heavy use of sanctions for a time is necessary to reinforce the seriousness of obligations. But if 40 percent of participants continue to receive sanctions each month, W-2 will have failed to meet perhaps its severest challenge — the exertion of an informal authority that encourages full participation among those most at risk.

The Use of Surplus Resources

In its first year of operation, W-2 cost much less than expected. In 1997-98, childcare expenditures were $71 million less than anticipated, and expenditures by W-2 agencies were about $98 million less than budgeted. The state keeps all unspent childcare funds and, through a formula contained in contracts with W-2 agencies, is likely to recapture some $37 million of their underspending. The contracts specify that W-2 agencies may retain the remaining surplus — $25 million for the agencies' unrestricted use, and $36 million for "reinvestment in the community for services to low-income persons," subject to state approval (Wisconsin Legislative Fiscal Bureau 1998). Many suggestions — from tax relief, to additional services for W-2 participants with drug-abuse problems, to more education for W-2 participants — have surfaced for the use of these funds, but decisions have not yet been made.

Information Systems

Wisconsin's public assistance information system (Client Assistance for Re-employment and Economic Support, or CARES) was originally designed primarily to determine AFDC eligibility and benefits. As others have noted (Wiseman 1997), information requirements in a program like W-2, which emphasizes progression through the rungs, are quite different from those of AFDC, which emphasized a condition — eligible or not in a particular month for a particular level of AFDC benefits. One would thus expect the state to experience some difficulty in adjusting CARES for W-2.

One of the system's virtues is the large volume of data it collects. CARES was designed to promote online, interactive information gathering, in which economic support workers entered data as they asked families questions to determine eligibility and benefits for AFDC. Because these characteristics continue under W-2, much information goes into a central state database. This continuation did not happen automatically. Private W-2 agencies sought to develop and maintain their own data systems without the overhead of a common state system, but the state stood its ground, requiring the use of CARES in all agency contracts. The database can report how long people remain at various levels of W-2, the services that individuals receive, their number of months of remaining eligibility, the characteristics of people who are sanctioned, and much other useful information. Urban W-2 agencies have access to automated online reports and weekly and monthly data files extracted from CARES, which also offers an online query system.

But though CARES collects masses of data, it also fails to gather some that would be potentially useful for W-2 managers and evaluators, such as the particular unsubsidized jobs that participants obtain and the stability of their employment. Data matches with the state Unemployment Insurance system can compensate for some, though by no means all, of these gaps. A more important problem is that some useful routine reports that the system could provide are sometimes not available owing to a lack of programming resources and the rush of new policies under W-2. Nine months after the initiation of W-2, decisions were still being made about what constituted a W-2 "case" in the data system,[8] and literally dozens of useful routine reports remained to be programmed.

CARES has more than 500 different screens and is not easy to learn to use. Times of great change (such as during the transition to W-2) and the efforts of new workers tend to generate "ad hoc" data entry, making the information in CARES something of a challenge to interpret. Analysis of a weekly activity report in April 1999 suggests that individual agencies have different rules of thumb for workers to use in coding information in CARES. Agencies and workers also express concern that data entered for one purpose might be used inappropriately for other purposes. Some agencies or individual FEPs, for example, have not entered wage rates and hours of employment on CARES screens, owing to concern that the information could identify food stamp calculation errors, which carry a financial penalty for the state and the agency. To cope with perceived weaknesses in routine CARES reports, some agencies have developed other tracking systems that include data downloaded from CARES coupled with other information.

Nevertheless, the CARES system offers much useful data, especially in comparison with some other states. Managers are seeking to improve the routine reports available from CARES and maintain its data richness while also simplifying the system so that W-2 staff and agencies do not develop their own *ad hoc* simplifications.

Staff Training

At the outset of W-2, the state established training requirements for JOBS and county economic support staff who wished to become FEPs or other W-2 staff members. The state required about one work month of training for staff to make the transition. Newly hired staff must complete a more intensive course, and all staff must fulfill 12 hours of professional development annually.

Because many W-2 staff have much discretion in their daily work with participants, careful staff training is important. It is also a challenge. FEPs spend a major part of their day, including during meetings with program participants, either entering or retrieving data from the CARES information system, which demands significant training time. Developing a good understanding of W-2 requirements and policies, community resources, general welfare-to-work strategies, and specific approaches for more difficult cases requires further training and experience. With all that FEPs have to learn, it is perhaps not surprising that, at least in the early months of W-2, some state policies escaped their attention. The child-support pass-through experiment, in which some W-2 participants receive all the child support paid on their behalf and others receive only some, provides an example. For the experiment to be a valid test of the impact of the new policy, FEPs must explain the child support policy applying to each participant. The following partial transcript of an interview in February 1998 with a Milwaukee FEP is reasonably representative of the status of FEP training, at least in Milwaukee, on this topic:

FEP: [The CARES computer system] might tell us this person has been selected for the control group. But I never tell them that they have been selected because I really don't know. We don't have a screen that we can just look in there and it will show, that's what I'm saying.

INTERVIEWER: So you don't have a screen that tells you that?

FEP: I mean there might be a screen in there, but we're not familiar with it. But I just tell them to go forward [with obtaining as much child support as possible], you know. Every little bit helps.

INTERVIEWER: Do you talk about it at all with them, that some people are in this group and some are in this? Or do you just leave that to the Child Support staff?

FEP: I tell them that, you know, because sometimes they asked "Are they going to get the full amount," or "Could they?" Because they, a lot of times clients hear from other people and everything, and I tell them "Yeah, but I don't know what group you will fall up under." You know, I tell them, the only thing I could tell them is just, you know, "You'll be notified as to if you will get the whole amount opposed to part of it anyways." You know, because I can't tell them who will, because, I don't know. But they, you know, I don't talk to them about it.

INTERVIEWER: How will they get notified? Do you know?

FEP: I have no idea.[9]

In a major new initiative like W-2, the child-support experiment must have seemed relatively minor to FEPs. The purpose of citing this interview is not to belittle the knowledge of the FEP (there is, in fact, a CARES screen that would tell the FEP whether the participant was in the full or partial pass-through group), but to demonstrate the challenge FEPs faced in assimilating a mass of new information. The child support program is a small part of many changes in policy and practice. Given the size of the overall challenge, the resources invested in training have been modest.

Evaluating W-2

Evaluating W-2 has become something of a cottage industry. In November 1997, at a conference in Racine, Wisconsin, academic researchers, staff of independent evaluation firms, W-2 agency staff, and advocates set out to organize and integrate the various evaluation efforts then under way. The range of projects being entertained was impressive. Here, I describe only evaluations of W-2 formally endorsed by the state's Management and Evaluation Project (MEP). Governor Thompson created the MEP by proclamation, appointing several state agency staff (the chair is Jean Rogers, head of the Division of Economic Assistance) along with two outside researchers: Michael Wiseman of the Urban Institute, who serves as vice-chair, and Lawrence Mead of New York University. The governor also appointed a National Technical Advisory Committee to advise the MEP on evaluation concerns. Wiseman and Mead both serve on the technical advisory committee as well as on the MEP. Other members of the technical advisory group are:

Learning from the Leaders:
Welfare Reform and Policy in Five Midwestern States

- ❖ Eugene Bardach, University of California — Berkeley
- ❖ Henry E. Brady, University of California — Berkeley
- ❖ George Cave, Child Trends, Inc.
- ❖ Anna Kondratas, Urban Institute
- ❖ Larry Martin, University of Wisconsin — Milwaukee
- ❖ Rebecca Maynard, University of Pennsylvania
- ❖ Ronald Mincy, Ford Foundation
- ❖ Demetra Nightingale, Urban Institute
- ❖ John Weicher, Hudson Institute

The MEP has actively stimulated some evaluation projects, although it more typically reviews and sponsors proposals from others. The MEP has so far endorsed 17 evaluation projects, ranging from assessments of Wisconsin reforms that preceded W-2, to a study of W-2 implementation in Milwaukee, to projects using administrative data for evaluation, to surveys of people entering or leaving W-2. The projects are described in the appendix.

Only one of the evaluations, the study of the full pass-through of child-support payments, assesses impact by comparing treatment and control groups. In general, the MEP has not promoted the use of evaluations that have experimental design, owing in part to the experience of state officials in experimental evaluations of precursors to W-2. In some of those evaluations, county staff negated random assignment by excusing people from program requirements, and inadequate programming of the CARES system also interfered. A large policy change like W-2 may pose even greater challenges to experimental evaluation. It is likely, for example, that a program designed in part to change the message government conveys about the relative desirability of cash grants and jobs could not be broadly effective without "contaminating" a control group still receiving AFDC. No perfect alternative to experimental design has emerged for evaluating W-2. The large number of MEP-sponsored evaluation projects is partly an effort to try multiple approaches.

Only three of the projects have released formal reports so far. The survey of leavers from AFDC and W-2 in 1998 (Wisconsin Department of Workforce Development 1999) found that about 60 percent of respondents were employed six months after exit, and 17 percent had never been employed since leaving welfare. Of those working or who had worked since leaving public assistance, 77 percent worked at least 40 hours per week. About 68 percent of respondents described their financial condition as "just barely making it," and 48 percent said they had more money off welfare than when they were on the program.

The study of leavers from AFDC (Cancian et al. 1999) found that, among people who left the Wisconsin AFDC program in 1995-96, about two-thirds reported earnings to the Wisconsin Unemployment Insurance system in each of the first five calendar quarters after exit from AFDC. Women with more education and who were below age 40 were more likely to work. Among women who remained continuously off AFDC during the five quarters of observation, median annual earnings were about $9,100, and increased by over 2 percent. While the work effort of leavers and the growth in their earnings was impressive, relatively few were able to escape poverty over the first five quarters; even those who left AFDC and did not return had only about a 25 percent probability of escaping poverty. More than half of all leavers did not attain the income level they had received just before they left AFDC; that is, within the five quarters of observation, the decline in their welfare benefits more than offset their earnings increases.

The child-support demonstration evaluation generates quarterly reports on W-2 as well as on child-support payments and receipts (for example, Bartfeld, Cancian, and Meyer 1998). The quarterly reports have so far found that W-2 participants were more likely to move to higher rungs or off the program than to lower rungs, particularly for W-2 participants who reside outside of Milwaukee County.

Conclusion

W-2 is unique in its immediate work requirement, emphasis on the obligations of program participants rather than program providers, full pass-through of child support, and use of private agencies. The program is quite small, however, having enrolled many fewer cash and employment assistance participants than anticipated. If W-2 provides an example of "welfare as we may come to know it," then welfare will apparently be a small program.

The key impacts of W-2 more likely lie outside than inside the program. Wisconsin offers substantial childcare and health insurance support to families not enrolled in W-2 cash or employment assistance, in the hope that such supports will help families move into and up the labor market. Evaluations of the economic status of families who left Wisconsin's public assistance programs suggest that many find jobs in a very prosperous economy and that earnings increase with time off welfare, but income remains quite low and few escape poverty for at least five quarters after exit. The economic condition of families who would have enrolled in AFDC but did not enroll in W-2 cash and employment assistance remains to be explored. Findings on other potential impacts of W-2, such as child health status, are also not yet available. With its unique features, W-2 may offer, as its designers hope, a model for welfare reform. But it remains a model with uncertain impacts.

References

Aukofer, Frank A. 1996. Weakland Opposes W-2 Program; Archbishop Makes Plea for Children. *Milwaukee Journal Sentinel*, July 5, 1.

Bardach, Eugene. 1997. Implementing a Paternalist Welfare-to-Work Program. In *The New Paternalism: Supervisory Approaches to Poverty*, Lawrence M. Mead, ed. Washington, DC: Brookings Institution.

Bartfeld, Judi, Maria Cancian, and Daniel R. Meyer. 1998. Wisconsin Child Support Demonstration Evaluation: Quarterly Impact Report, Quarter 3. Madison, WI: Institute for Research on Poverty.

Bloom, Dan, Mary Farrell, James J. Kemple, and Nandita Verma. 1998. The Family Transition Program: Implementation and Interim Impact of Florida's Initial Time-Limited Welfare Program. New York: Manpower Demonstration Research Corp.

Bureau of Welfare Initiatives. 1998. W-2 Sanctions, October 1998. Madison, WI: Wisconsin Department of Workforce Development.

Butler, Stuart, and Anna Kondratas. 1987. *Out of the Poverty Trap: A Conservative Strategy for Welfare Reform*. New York: Free Press.

Cancian, Maria, and Robert Haveman, Thomas Kaplan, and Barbara Wolfe. 1999. Post-Exit Earnings and Benefit Receipt among

Those Who Left AFDC in Wisconsin. Madison, WI: Institute for Research on Poverty, Special Report #75.

Corbett, Thomas J. 1995. Welfare Reform in Wisconsin: The Rhetoric and the Reality. In *The Politics of Welfare Reform*, Donald F. Norris and Lyke Thompson, eds. Thousand Oaks, CA: Sage.

DeParle, Jason. 1998. Flaws Emerge in Wisconsin's Welfare-To-Work Plan. *The New York Times*, October 17.

Dresang, Joel. 1996. Thompson Announces Program to Promote Child Care. *Milwaukee Journal Sentinel*, July 25, 1.

Dresang, Joel. 1998. State Money Aims to Ease W-2 Troubles. *Milwaukee Journal Sentinel*, October 15, 1B.

Flaherty, Mike. 1998. Should Welfare Help Educate Its Recipients? *Wisconsin State Journal* (Madison), February 27, 1.

Folk, Karen Fox. 1996. Welfare Reform under Construction: Wisconsin Works (W-2). *Focus* 18(1): 55-57, Institute for Research on Poverty, University of Wisconsin — Madison.

Gillette, Michael L. 1996. *Launching the War on Poverty: An Oral History*. New York: Twayne Publishers.

Huston, Margo. 1998a. State Wants Tougher W-2 Enforcement. *Milwaukee Journal Sentinel*, January 22, B1.

Huston, Margo. 1998b. Agencies Urge Lawmakers to Alter W-2. *Milwaukee Journal Sentinel*, September 16, B1.

Huston, Margo. 1998c. State's Private Agencies First in U.S. to Receive Profits. *Milwaukee Journal Sentinel*, November 18, B1.

Jones, Richard P. 1996. Governor Demands Apology from Weakland. *Milwaukee Journal Sentinel*, July 9, 1.

Mead, Lawrence M. 1986. *Beyond Entitlement: The Social Obligations of Citizenship*. New York: Free Press.

Mead, Lawrence M. 1992. *The New Politics of Poverty: The Nonworking Poor in America*. New York: Basic Books.

Mead, Lawrence M. 1997. Welfare Employment. In *The New Paternalism: Supervisory Approaches to Poverty*, L.M. Mead, ed. Washington, DC: Brookings Institution.

Mead, Lawrence M. 1999. Statecraft: The Politics of Welfare Reform in Wisconsin. Madison, WI: Institute for Research on Poverty, Discussion Paper #1184-99.

Stingl, Jim. 1997. W-2's Toughest Test Awaits: Milwaukee. *Milwaukee Journal Sentinel*, May 18, 6S.

Office of the Wisconsin Governor. 1998. Governor Taps National Experts to Help Evaluate W-2. October 5.

U.S. Bureau of the Census. 1975. *Statistical Abstract of the United States*, 96th Ed. Washington, DC: U.S. Government Printing Office.

U.S. Bureau of the Census. 1997. *Statistical Abstract of the United States* (117th Edition). Washington, DC: U.S. Government Printing Office.

U.S. Department of Health and Human Services, Office of Child Support Enforcement. 1997. *Child Support Report*. Washington, DC: Department of Health and Human Services, December.

U.S. House of Representatives, Committee on Ways and Means. 1992. *Overview of Entitlement Programs: 1992 Green Book*. Washington, DC: U.S. Government Printing Office.

Wisconsin Department of Health and Social Services. 1995. *Wisconsin Works*. Madison, WI.: Department of Health and Social Services.

Wisconsin Department of Workforce Development. 1997a. *Rules in Final Draft Form: DWD-12, Wisconsin Works*. Madison, WI: Department of Workforce Development.

Wisconsin Department of Workforce Development. 1997b. *Wisconsin Works Policy*. Madison, WI: Department of Workforce Development.

Wisconsin Department of Workforce Development. 1998. *Wisconsin Works Manual* Release 98-03. Madison, WI: Department of Workforce Development, October.

Wisconsin Department of Workforce Development. 1999. *Survey of Those Leaving AFDC or W-2 January to March 1998: Preliminary Report.* Madison, WI: Department of Workforce Development.

Wisconsin Legislative Fiscal Bureau. 1997. Wisconsin Works: W-2. Madison, WI: Legislative Fiscal Bureau.

Wisconsin Legislative Fiscal Bureau. 1998. Unexpended Funding under the Agency Contracts for the Wisconsin Works (W-2) Program and from the Child Care Program. Memorandum, November 3.

Wiseman, Michael. 1996. State Strategies for Welfare Reform: The Wisconsin Story. *Journal of Policy Analysis and Management* 15: 515-546.

Wiseman, Michael. 1997. A Management Information System for Wisconsin Works. *Evaluating Comprehensive Welfare Reforms: A Conference.* Madison, WI: Institute for Research on Poverty, Special Report #69.

Witte, Edwin E. 1963. *The Development of the Social Security Act.* Madison, WI: University of Wisconsin Press.

APPENDIX

Evaluation Projects Sponsored by the Wisconsin Department of
Workforce Development Management Evaluation Plan

1. *Wisconsin Public Assistance Database (WISPAD).* This project merges files on individual families across administrative sources (such as the CARES system, the child welfare information system, and the Unemployment Insurance system) and across years. A goal is to protect family confidentiality but allow limited access by researchers. This is a joint project of the Wisconsin Department of Workforce Development and Institute for Research on Poverty (IRP) at the University of Wisconsin-Madison.

2. *Self-Sufficiency First/Pay for Performance.* This evaluation, conducted by IRP researchers, attempts to measure the impact of the programs, which operated as transitions to W-2 starting in March 1996. For the first 14 months of these projects, participants in four counties were randomly assigned to treatment and control groups.

3. *Implementation of W-2 in Milwaukee.* In cooperation with the Department of Workforce Development, the Manpower Demonstration Research Corporation (MDRC) is conducting a study of the early implementation of W-2 among the five private agencies administering the program in Milwaukee.

4. *Expansion of the National Survey of America's Families in Wisconsin.* The state has secured foundation funding for expanding the Wisconsin sample size of this survey, which is being conducted by the Urban Institute to gauge the effects of TANF. The sample is large enough to be representative of Milwaukee County as well as the state as a whole.

5. *IRP Survey of Milwaukee Families Who Contact W-2 Agencies.* This survey, conducted with resources from the Joyce Foundation and the U.S. Department of Health and Human Services, will

survey 1,000 Milwaukee families after their initial contacts with W-2 agencies and again one year later.

6. *Hudson Institute and Mathematica Policy Research Survey of Families Leaving or Avoiding AFDC in Milwaukee.* This survey effort is an attempt to better understand the reasons for and impacts of the large AFDC caseload decline that occurred in Milwaukee before the start of W-2.

7. *AFDC Baseline.* This study by IRP researchers uses administrative data to study the labor market and income progression of AFDC participants in the early 1990s.

8. *Study of Leavers from W-2.* This continuing study, being conducted by DWD staff, uses administrative data and a questionnaire to better understand the motivations and well-being of families who leave the W-2 program.

9. *Leavers from AFDC.* This study by IRP researchers uses administrative data to assess the labor force participation, earnings, and incomes of the full population of single, adult women who left AFDC between July 1995 and June 1996.

10. *Child Support Waiver Demonstration Project.* This IRP study evaluates the impact of the full pass-through of child support to families under W-2. Some families were randomly assigned to the full pass-through, and others to a reduced pass-through.

11. *Children First.* This DWD study examines the effects of the Children First program, which required noncustodial parents in child support payment arrears to participate in various job search activities or face further legal penalties. The program operated between 1994 and 1996. Participants in one county were assigned to control and experimental status.

12. *Experiences of Dane County W-2 Participants.* This longitudinal study, conducted by IRP, uses administrative data and a two-wave survey to understand experiences of new applicants to W-2 and participants who transferred to W-2 from AFDC. The study is funded by the U.S. Department of Health and Human Services, the Joyce Foundation, and the University of Wisconsin.

13. *Milwaukee Employer Survey.* Under the direction of Harry Holzer of Michigan State University, this is a survey of 750 employers in Milwaukee to examine their need for, and experience with, TANF participants and their willingness to hire them. A similar survey is underway in Chicago, Cleveland, Los Angeles and Detroit/Flint.

14. *New Hope Evaluation.* This is an evaluation by MDRC of a pilot work-based antipoverty program operated in Milwaukee during the mid-1990s.

15. *Linked Administrative Data: CARES and the Human Services Reporting System (HSRS).* With funding from the U.S. Department of Health and Human Services, IRP is studying the linking of Wisconsin HSRS data (which contains foster care and other child welfare and human services data) to CARES.

16. *Team Parenting Demonstration.* This project, in Racine County, is one of eight around the country being evaluated by the federal Office of Child Support Enforcement. The program provides services to noncustodial parents in an effort to improve paternity establishment and increase child support and nonfinancial support for their children.

17. *Head Start Collaboration Study.* Conducted by the University of Wisconsin-Milwaukee Center for Economic Development, this study (a) interviews low-income working parents about childcare and (b) surveys current and former Head Start participants about experiences with W-2.

Endnotes

1   Other states have apparently presented time limits differently. An evalua-tion by the Manpower Demonstration Research Corporation in one Florida County found that program participants cited time limits as the least im-portant factor in their decision to seek a job. The largest proportion of re-spondents—nearly half—said their decision to seek a job had been strongly influenced by the availability of support services such as childcare. Recipients also generally rated the availability of employment and training services, advice and assistance from staff, and financial incen-tives as more important than time limits in their job search motivation. These responses were consistent with group discussions held with partici-pants, many of whom "were focused on day-to-day problems, and saw the time limit as a distant concern" (Bloom et al. 1998). Still, as the authors of that report noted, time limits may have larger impacts in other settings. Florida provided low AFDC benefits, so the consequences of losing bene-fits were not as severe, and county staff did not stress saving available months for a time when participants might need them more. The primary message of the Florida limits was that participants should use their avail-able time to develop skills likely to help them obtain better positions in the future. Time limits may have greater motivational impact in a state where staff emphasize saving limited months for future contingencies.

2   Under current W-2 administrative procedures, the financial and employ-ment planner must take action to impose a penalty; the W-2 case manage-ment computer system does not automatically reduce benefits for hours missed.

3   The Job Opportunities and Basic Skills Training program (JOBS) was mandated by the Family Support Act of 1988.

4   For 1971—1974, for example, the national and Wisconsin unemployment rates were: 1971, 5.9 percent (U.S.) and 4.5 percent (WI); 1972, 5.6 per-cent (U.S.) and 4.3 percent (WI); 1973, 4.9 percent (U.S.) and 4.0 percent (WI); 1974, 5.6 percent (U.S.) and 4.5 percent (WI) (U.S. Bureau of the Census 1975). By comparison, the 1996 unemployment rates were 5.4 per-cent (U.S.) and 3.8 percent (WI) (U.S. Bureau of the Census 1997).

5   The focus groups were conducted by Elisabeth Boehnen and Thomas Corbett at the Institute for Research on Poverty, University of Wiscon-sin–Madison, under a project titled Marketplace Analysis: Matching Skills and Opportunities—Welfare to Work.

6   Some W-2 agencies have responded to concerns about difficulties with telephone contact by requiring that FEPs answer calls as they come in, even if another participant is in the FEP's office.

7   The number of cases in sanction status, and the percentage of all cases these represented, were: July 1998, 2,801 cases (25.7 percent); August

1998, 2,963 cases (29.2 percent); September 1998, 2,667 cases (26.7 percent). Mean sanction amounts for the three months were July, $354; August, $346; and September, $431 (Bureau of Welfare Initiatives 1998).

8   The complexities of counting a case have at least two origins. First, CARES as it operated under AFDC required that each case be entered into an assistance group subsystem for each month of eligibility. The system was designed so as not to generate an AFDC check unless the case was in the subsystem. Thus, when management information analysts sought to determine the total number of AFDC cases, they could obtain an accurate number from this subsystem. Under W-2, however, systems programmers removed the edit requiring entry into the assistance group subsystem before eligibility was granted. For reasons that are unclear, the management information programmers were unaware of this change in system policy. They continued to count program totals from the subsystem, thereby undercounting by some 5 percent the number of W-2 cases actually receiving services or a grant.

A second issue complicating case counts has involved cases in the unsubsidized job level whose income is greater than the theoretical maximum W-2 income of 115 percent of the federal poverty line. Particularly if the participant starts in a lower level of W-2 and then graduates into a job paying more than 115 percent of the poverty line, it has not been clear whether the case continues as a W-2 case for at least the six months of required follow-up, or whether the case should not be counted in W-2 because it exceeds the 115 percent threshold.

9   Victoria Mayer and I conducted this interview in February 1998, as part of an evaluation of the child-support pass-through policy.

Chapter 5

MINNESOTA'S BALANCING ACT: BOOSTING WORK INCENTIVES AND JOB READINESS WHILE CONTROLLING COSTS

Thomas F. Luce, Jr.

When the U.S. Congress passed the Personal Responsibility and Work Opportunity Reconciliation Act of 1996, Minnesota was relatively well placed to respond to the requirements of the new program. The Minnesota economy had performed well for more than a decade — the 1991 recession lasted just one quarter in Minnesota, and the state economy has consistently outperformed the national economy ever since. The state had already been experimenting with welfare-to-work initiatives on several fronts, both with its federally mandated JOBS program (Success through Reaching Individual Development and Employment, or STRIDE), and with a pilot initiative (the Minnesota Family Investment Program, or MFIP). The state had also put other important initiatives in place to complement welfare-to-work initiatives. These included a health insurance program targeted at the working poor (reducing the incentive for families to stay on welfare to continue health care coverage), and a sliding-scale childcare program available to non-welfare and near-poor families. Finally, political actors had come to widespread agreement on the basic structure of new welfare legislation.

The resulting welfare program passed in April 1997, well before any federally mandated deadlines. Officially known as MFIP-S, the program's design borrows from at least three programs with distinct philosophies: the traditional AFDC program, which focused largely on controlling costs in the context of an entitlement program with a diverse clientele; STRIDE, which emphasized intensive services to a relatively small, self-selected group; and MFIP, which combined financial incentives and mandatory job search, education, and training activities for a relatively wide cross section of recipients.

The final design (designated by TANF hereafter to distinguish it from the MFIP demonstration) owes more to AFDC and MFIP than to STRIDE. It attempts to boost the incentives and reduce the disincentives to work inherent in the old AFDC system while also de-emphasizing intensive and expensive education and training activities that prepare participants for more productive employment. Overall benefit levels most resemble AFDC; the case management philosophy and the treatment of food stamps and outside income most resemble MFIP. The balance among education, training, and job search activities is a hybrid, with more emphasis on transition to work than AFDC but less emphasis on relatively intensive (and expensive) education and training activities than MFIP or STRIDE.

Although it is still too early to evaluate the effects of this approach in encouraging transition from welfare to work, some troubling indicators are emerging, including a wide range of funding for county-level education and training activities as well as rising and widely varying sanction rates. Thus Minnesota's experience so far provides some clues about the potential long-run outcome of welfare reform but cannot yet provide reliable indicators of the overall viability of TANF.

The Origins of TANF

The process of restructuring Minnesota's welfare system began in the fall of 1996, immediately after passage of the national TANF program. The governor and state legislative leaders made it clear that their intent was to model Minnesota's new welfare system on the MFIP demonstration project, in which the state had invested a great deal of time and resources spanning two gubernatorial administrations. Democratic Governor Rudy Perpich launched the MFIP planning process in 1989 by appointing a task force with a broad mandate to address welfare dependency. The group, composed of legislators, human services administrators, and representatives of organizations such as Catholic Charities and Save the Children, developed the MFIP model. The program was initially implemented in April 1994 as a pilot project in 7 of Minnesota's 87 counties.

MFIP, loosely patterned on the much-publicized program from Riverside County, Calif., was designed to reduce the financial disincentives to leave welfare.[1] The system was also simplified by combining AFDC and food stamp benefits into a single monthly check. Participants who had received welfare for two or more years were required to either pursue work directly or be enrolled in any of a relatively wide range of training activities. When they found employment, recipients continued to receive childcare and health care services as well as a cash grant to the point where their total income (welfare plus wages) exceeded 140 percent of the poverty line. The original demonstration program did not emphasize sanctions, but parents who did not cooperate with the job search or education components could see their benefits cut by up to 10 percent.

An evaluation of MFIP by the Manpower Demonstration Research Corporation tracked 9,000 individuals randomly assigned to either MFIP or traditional AFDC programs (Miller et al. 1997). The study found that the combination of financial incentives and mandatory employment, training, and job search activities did increase employment rates and family income for long-term recipients in urban areas. MFIP participants in this category were 39 percent more likely to be employed after 16-18 months in the program, and their private earnings and total income were 27 and 13 percent higher, respectively, than similar recipients in the AFDC control group. As a result, the percentage of these MFIP families with incomes below the poverty line was about 16 percent lower than for their AFDC counterparts. But although long-term recipients from urban areas were more likely to be earning private income, they also received about 8 percent more in public benefits than their AFDC counterparts (because of the greater income disregard and a greater propensity to combine welfare with work). MFIP clearly cost more per case than AFDC, at least in the short run.

The study also found that the combination of mandatory participation and financial incentives was important. MFIP participants in urban areas who received the augmented financial incentives without any required education, training, or job search activities did not show significantly higher private earnings than their AFDC counterparts, and their employment rates were only marginally higher. This group was also more likely to stay on welfare than AFDC participants, and received benefits that averaged 14 percent higher.

The impacts of MFIP on other groups — new applicants in urban areas and long-term recipients in rural areas — were less impressive. MFIP participants in these groups showed no significant increases in employment rates after 16-18 months, and no improvement in private earnings relative to their AFDC counterparts. They were also more likely to remain on welfare (at higher benefit levels) than the control group.

MFIP did lead to significant improvements for the group of welfare participants long regarded as the most difficult to serve — long-term recipients in urban areas. This is, of course, the largest cohort of recipients in many states, including Minnesota, where more than 50 percent of welfare recipients reside in Hennepin and Ramsey counties, which contain Minneapolis and St. Paul. Since TANF requires education and training activities for all participants, and since the largest numbers of affected recipients are in the Twin Cities metropolitan area, 1997 discussion of the new reforms emphasized the results for long-term urban recipients.[2] But the program was also more expensive (at least in the short run) than traditional AFDC, and it did not show the desired effects on employment and private earnings for relatively large components of the welfare population. The effects of the more intensive education and training services provided by MFIP might also have abated after the 18-month period covered by the study. A follow-up study scheduled for release in 1999 will examine such longer-run effects. In any case, the MFIP experience clearly shows that the approach is not a magic bullet that solves all problems for all participants.

STRIDE, the other major welfare initiative relevant for TANF, was implemented in 1989 and emphasized education- and training-based strategies to increase the long-run earning capacity of participants. Case management focused on early assessment of clients, the development of an employment plan, and referral to services. Participation in most STRIDE activities was voluntary: The only mandatory components were an orientation for all AFDC recipients introducing them to the program, attendance in school (or a high school diploma program) for parents under the age of 20 without a degree, and participation in job search activities for the principal wage earner in two-parent AFDC families.[3]

The MFIP and STRIDE experiences meant that Minnesota entered the TANF era with a relatively diverse menu of potential program designs available to legislators. What eventually emerged borrowed components from both of these programs, as well as from the state's traditional AFDC program.

The Politics of Minnesota's Program Design

In January 1997, Republican Governor Arne Carlson appointed a bipartisan task force composed of legislators and officials from the Department of Human Services (DHS) to develop recommendations for system-wide welfare reform. After holding a number of meetings, the task force produced draft legislation that was the subject of House and Senate hearings in March of 1997. The final TANF bill was passed and signed by the governor at the end of April 1997.

Considering the historic nature of the reforms, the debate in the legislature and public forums was remarkably free of controversy, and passage of the bill remarkably rapid. The legislature and the governor agreed on the major stated objective — greater emphasis on moving people from welfare to work in a way that would decrease poverty but that would not break the bank. There was general agreement on building a TANF policy based not only on MFIP but also on other state programs such as MinnesotaCare, the program that provides health insurance to lower-income individuals and families who do not qualify for Medicaid and who do not have access to health insurance through their employers. A sliding-fee childcare program also provides daycare subsidies to working-poor families, although the program has been underfunded since its inception and thus has long waiting lists.

Both the administration and the legislature avoided negative rhetoric about welfare recipients. The negativity that did exist was primarily directed at welfare recipients who had recently moved to Minnesota from other states. Since Minnesota has a tradition of providing relatively generous welfare benefits, many in the state legislature and the public have perceived the state as a "welfare magnet." This perception led directly to provisions in the new law intended to reduce benefits to new state residents for their first year — provisions that are not being enforced until they work their way through the inevitable court challenges.[4]

The strength of Minnesota's economy in the 1990s also played a significant role in shaping the conceptions of state policymakers. For the last several years the state has had an unemployment rate below 5 percent, and most recently it dropped to record levels below 3 percent. (In the Twin Cities metropolitan area, the unemployment rate reached as low as 2.2 percent during several months in 1997 and 1998.) Employers and economists have noted a labor shortage in many sectors of the state's economy. This strong economic climate motivated legislators who might not otherwise do so, such as liberal Democrats, to favor a TANF program with a strong focus on work.

The Governor and the Administration

Republican Governor Arne Carlson and members of the administration stated from the beginning that their goal was to create a less expensive system that placed more emphasis on moving recipients into jobs. They pushed for adoption of the MFIP model combined with de-emphasis of the commitment to long-term education and training that was the core of STRIDE (a program that the governor argued had been ineffective). Welfare reform also offered Carlson the perfect vehicle to continue his support of the state's most important non-AFDC anti-poverty programs (MinnesotaCare and the sliding-scale childcare program).

The Legislature

The Minnesota House and Senate were both controlled by the Democratic-Farmer-Labor Party (DFL) at the time of TANF debate and passage. Most DFL legislators strongly supported MFIP, MinnesotaCare, and the childcare program, so the governor's basic framework raised relatively few objections. However, the final bill was slightly tougher regarding work requirements and benefit levels but more generous to legal immigrants and disabled children than the governor's proposals. These changes responded to legislative hearings in which various groups sought to restore federal cuts in AFDC and Social Security benefits for legal immigrants and disabled individuals — changes supported by a relatively large block of moderate Democrats and nearly all Republicans.[5]

Counties and Other Local Governments

Minnesota's welfare delivery system is a state-supervised, county-administered system with significant powers decentralized to lower levels of government. Throughout the debate over welfare reform, counties sought more freedom from some state rules regarding diversion assistance (short-term support to TANF applicants provided to help them avoid enrollment in TANF) and the design and development of job training programs, but in the end the division of powers changed little. The state sets stipend levels and the overall structure of the program, while counties determine the mix of education and training services they offer, case management strategies (including, within limits, sanctions policies), and the extent to which services are provided in-house or through contracts with nonprofits.

Some counties, including Hennepin County (the state's most populous), pushed the legislature to cut benefits from MFIP levels, arguing that maintaining benefits at those relatively high levels could make it difficult to meet the stricter TANF requirements for moving recipients into jobs. Hennepin County was also concerned that relatively liberal exemption rules (for mothers with children younger than one year, for instance) could absolve up to 40 percent of recipients from work requirements, making it difficult to meet federal transition-to-work targets.

Hennepin and other counties also expressed concern that if the new law allowed greater diversity among welfare plans, counties might be forced to use local property tax revenue to assist poor families, potentially creating "county welfare magnets." Other local governments, chiefly cities with large immigrant and poor populations such as Minneapolis and St. Paul, expressed concern that their schools and social services would be disproportionately affected by the new program.

Nonprofit Agencies, Labor, and Businesses

Nonprofit secular and religious social service agencies worried that they would be unable to fully replace long-run cuts in federal support if the economy faltered. Their primary focus was the time limits proposed by the national law, and they were influential in the decision to exempt parents providing full-time care for a child less than one year old from TANF work requirements. The law limits this exemption to a total of 12 months over the lifetime of the custodial parent. (The exemption may be spread over several children but still totals 12 months.)

Immigrant groups convinced the state to replace a portion of legal immigrants' food stamps eliminated by federal TANF legislation. The state's modest program, Minnesota Grown, provides up to $40 per person per month to immigrant households that previously received food stamps. Clients must use the vouchers to purchase food products grown or produced in Minnesota, and county participation is voluntary.

A number of welfare advocacy groups participated in the debate, largely in opposition to the changes. The Welfare Rights Committee presented the strongest opposition to TANF. On numerous occasions this group demonstrated outside the capital building to protest the bill and opposed any cuts or changes in the state's welfare system. State legislators later suggested that these groups exerted little influence, and that in fact their protests may have alienated some legislators who might otherwise have supported their positions.

Immediately after passage of the TANF legislation, the McKnight Foundation, a philanthropic organization headquartered in the Twin Cities, pledged $20 million in grants to state and community organizations to develop "local support networks" to coordinate education, training, childcare, and transportation. The initiative is designed to complement the state's welfare reform effort by building welfare-to-work community partnerships, especially in parts of the state where they do not exist. McKnight estimates that it will eventually fund 26 planning grants ranging from $5,500 to $50,000 that involve community partnerships in every Minnesota county. Projects include a loan program to buy and maintain automobiles for welfare recipients and a program to ensure quality childcare in non-licensed settings. The foundation is also considering projects that would provide TANF recipients, especially those in rural Minnesota, with transportation to jobs.

Owing to a labor shortage in most of the state, many employers professed a willingness in hearings to hire and train welfare recipients, and businesses have actively worked with county welfare agencies and local employment and training agencies to match welfare recipients with job openings. However, the real test will come when more participants are forced out of welfare by the new time limits, or when the economy slows.

Public employee unions were very involved in developing guidelines for the Community Work Experience Program (CWEP) and other employment programs for JOBS and AFDC recipients that imposed a minimum wage and limited the programs' use in state agencies. The result is that CWEP has been used very little in the state.[6] These guidelines did not change significantly in the TANF legislation, and unions were not a significant factor in the state's TANF effort.

Design Components of TANF

Although the MFIP demonstration provided the official template for TANF in Minnesota, the program that eventually emerged de-emphasized or eliminated some of MFIP's most prominent features. Since federal block grants under TANF will eventually involve funding that is less than or at best equal to the previous AFDC system, the challenge of making MFIP work with less money was a prominent issue. The eventual solution entailed reducing the cutoff point for support from 140 percent of the federal poverty level to 120 percent,[7] and shifting emphasis from expensive, long-term education and training services to much less expensive, shorter-term job search strategies.

Benefit Levels

Table 5-1 shows how benefit levels under TANF compare to those under AFDC and MFIP. Shown are monthly welfare grants, food stamps and total monthly income for a single parent with two children working part-time or full-time at the minimum wage. Also

	AFDC (1-5 mos.)	AFDC (5-12 mos.)	MFIP Demo	TANF
Table 5-1 **Comparison of Benefits for a Single Parent Family with Two Children: AFDC, MFIP Demonstration, and TANF**				
Working Twenty Hours per Week at Minimum Wage ($5.15)				
Monthly Wage	$443	$443	$443	$443
Monthly Grant	317	209	648	578
Food Stamps	195	227	—	—
Total Income	955	879	1,091	1,021
Total Income as % of Poverty Level	93	86	106	90
Hourly Wage at Exit from Program	16.14	16.27	17.31	16.79
Total Income at Exit as % of Poverty Level	136	136	145	128
Working Forty Hours per Week at Minimum Wage ($5.15)				
Monthly Wage	$886	$886	$886	$886
Monthly Grant	21	0	374	294
Food Stamps	176	184	—	—
Total Income	1,083	1,070	1,260	1,180
Total Income as % of Poverty Level	106	104	123	104
Hourly Wage at Exit from Program	8.13	8.13	8.66	8.16
Total Income at Exit as % of Poverty Level	136	136	145	128

AFDC and MFIP calculations are for 1994. TANF calculations are for 1998.
Food stamp calculations assume monthly shelter costs of $500 in 1994 and $563 in 1998 with no childcare costs.
Source: Minnesota Department of Human Services.

shown is the wage at which the household is no longer eligible for welfare benefits or food stamps. Two simulations are shown for AFDC because benefits under that program declined after the participant had been in the program for five months. (Another decline occurred after 12 months but Table 5-1 does not reflect that.)

Table 5-1 shows that benefit rates under TANF are roughly commensurate with those for AFDC and food stamps combined during the first five months of participation in AFDC, with one important difference: benefits decline more slowly with additional private income under TANF. For instance, under AFDC when private income grew from $0 to $443 per month (a half-time job at minimum wage), clients lost $257 in benefits ($215 of grant and $42 in food stamps). For each additional $1 of private income, AFDC clients lost roughly $.70 of benefits (about $.67 in welfare grant and $.03 in food stamps). Under TANF they lose just $204 in total benefits with the first $443 of private income, and just $.64 in benefits for each additional dollar of income.

Clients also remain eligible for a welfare stipend up to a higher total income under TANF (roughly 122 percent of the poverty level) than under AFDC (where welfare grants ended at about 107 percent of the poverty line). However, the food stamp program was more generous in years prior to 1998. The net result is that AFDC recipients remained eligible for some benefits up to 136 percent of the poverty line in 1994 compared with just 128 percent under TANF in 1998. (Once clients reach the maximum income for TANF benefits, which combine food stamps with welfare, they become eligible for a relatively small additional food stamp grant. Whether clients will actually take advantage of this limited benefit is debatable, but it is included in the calculations for Table 5-1.) Overall, benefits under TANF look much like those for AFDC during the first five months of participation. At lower income levels, TANF is a bit more generous and therefore more expensive after five months, and this difference is greater after 12 months (not shown in Table 5-1). In the long run, however, this additional cost may be offset as clients reach the five-year limit under federal law.[8]

Table 5-1 also shows that MFIP was clearly more generous (and costly) than either AFDC or TANF. Participants were eligible for assistance up to a higher level of income — 145 percent of the poverty line for this type of family. Although participants who did not work received a benefit commensurate with AFDC, benefits declined more slowly with each dollar of private income (at a rate of about $.61 per dollar of additional private income) than under AFDC or TANF.

Changes in the availability of education and training services under TANF also reflect a shift away from the original MFIP and STRIDE philosophy. Participants in MFIP and STRIDE could participate in up to 36 months of post-secondary education or training, but TANF has reduced this to just 12 months. Participants may continue education activities for an additional 12 months only if they agree to repay the state once their income exceeds 150 percent of the poverty line. Whether this approach can yield even the relatively modest outcomes of the MFIP demonstration remains to be seen.

Distribution of Funds

The state controls the two funding streams that support education and training in TANF: the MFIP-S Work Grants Program (MSWG) and the Welfare-to-Work Grants (W2W).[9] MSWG funds come from both federal (roughly 80 percent of the total) and state (about 20 percent) sources. MSWG funding for education and training activities in fiscal year 1999 was set at about $38 million. The state distributes funds to the counties according to a two-part formula based on the funds counties received for employment and training activities under STRIDE, and their average number of cases compared with the statewide average during two prior years. Both parts of this formula create the potential for inequities. Counties with a lower-than-average proportion of clients in the groups targeted by the STRIDE program receive less funding, despite the fact that TANF does not specifically target those groups. And because the formula relies on two-year-old caseload date, it cannot accommodate dramatic shifts in caseloads. This could be a problem if clients in various regions show differing propensities (or abilities) to leave welfare. Similarly, if economic conditions vary significantly across the rate (rural versus metropolitan, or city versus suburb), relative caseloads might change fairly rapidly. These features of the allocation formula have in fact resulted in significant funding inequities, as discussed below.

W2W funding for the first year of TANF totaled $14.5 million. The formula for distributing W2W funds, which are entirely federal, is based on broader categories and thus produces fewer clear inequities as measured by broad indicators of need. Some 50 percent of

W2W funding must be distributed based on the number of people in poverty above 7.5 percent. Minnesota distributes 25 percent of the remaining funds according to the number of TANF or AFDC clients who have received assistance for 30 months or more, and 25 percent according to the number of unemployed adults.

All TANF recipients are eligible for Minnesota's sliding fee childcare program. The program has been in existence since 1989 but has never received funds adequate to cover all eligible families. In conjunction with TANF, the legislature increased funds for the childcare program and made it a bit easier for less expensive non-licensed providers (often extended family members) to qualify. These changes allow guaranteed access to childcare support for welfare participants, but not to all eligible non-welfare households. Increases in 1999 raised funding to record levels and should reduce the waiting list for non-welfare households from about 7,000 to 4,000.[10] However, the fact that enrolling in welfare is the only way for a family to be guaranteed access is troubling, given that an important objective of welfare reform is to reduce the incentives for recipients to enter the system. Indeed, reports have surfaced that some parents are leaving jobs for welfare to gain access to childcare benefits.[11]

TANF also expanded, although only marginally, eligibility for transportation assistance. Participants in traditional AFDC were not eligible for such assistance, but under TANF they are eligible on a case-by-case basis, depending on the job search, education, or employment plan. Transportation assistance is particularly important in Minnesota, as rural commutes can involve significant distances and public transit is very limited. Transportation can be a problem even in the Twin Cities, which is one of the least densely settled large metropolitan areas in the country with one of the least-developed public transit systems. As in other states, most job growth is occurring in outer suburbs, exacerbating reliance on automobiles for commuting.

Case Management

TANF retains the basic case-management strategy developed in the MFIP demonstration and STRIDE. With assistance from a caseworker, TANF participants must develop one or more of four plans: a job search support plan, an employment plan, an educational progress and need plan, and a safety plan. The jobs of local staff who participated in MFIP and STRIDE have changed little: Those who worked largely with traditional AFDC clients have had to adjust to the new philosophy, but all workers had been exposed to some extent to the STRIDE or MFIP philosophies.

A recipient first meets with a job counselor to determine her/his ability to secure employment. This assessment must consider the recipient's education level, previous employment history, work skills, and the labor market. The job counselor and the recipient develop a plan that requires the recipient, if the job counselor determines that she or he is employable, to conduct an employment search at least 30 hours a week up to eight weeks. During the eight-week search, either the job counselor or recipient may ask for a review of the plan.

A more in-depth assessment must be performed if the eight-week job search is unsuccessful, if the recipient has significant barriers to finding employment, or if the recipient is working only 20 hours a week. This secondary assessment reexamines skills and prior work experience and also examines interests and family life. The job counselor then uses this information to develop an employment plan, which must specify activities that will lead to long-term self-sufficiency. Both recipient and counselor must sign this agreement.

Parents under the age of 20 must also complete an assessment of educational progress and need and agree to pursue an educational plan. Most parents below the age of 20 who have not received their high school diploma must attend school. If there is no educational option, the parent and the job counselor will develop an employment plan.

Sanctioning of clients who do not comply with TANF work or job search requirements is stricter than under prior programs. Under the law, parents who do not follow the rules lose 10 percent of their stipend in the first month and 30 percent in the second. The reduced stipend is sent directly to landlords; TANF recipients receive only the remainder after rent is paid.

Implementation Issues

Full-scale implementation of the new program, which began in January 1998, has already yielded some troublesome developments.

The most important are an uneven distribution of education and training funds among counties, significant and uneven jumps in sanction rates, underfunding of the sliding-fee childcare program for non-welfare recipients, and concern regarding the ability of the economy to absorb recipients leaving welfare.

Funding Inequities

A review of the county-by-county spending plans for the first year of TANF shows very wide variations in the availability of funds for education and training. For example, while average MSGW funding for the first year of TANF was $807 per case, the county-by-county funding ranged from a low of $579 to a high of $1,988.[12] Although a county-administered system is designed to accommodate local demographics and experiments, this range seems hard to justify. Hennepin County, which has the largest caseload and includes the city with the largest concentration of poverty (Minneapolis), receives an MSGW allocation ($715 per case) more than 10 percent below the statewide average. Meanwhile Ramsey County, which encompasses St. Paul, receives an allocation a bit above the average, at $867 per case.

W2W funding allocations do little to narrow the disparities. The statewide W2W average is $253 per case, with a range from $169 to $1,330. Hennepin County receives the second-lowest allocation from this program ($171 per case), while Ramsey County is only slightly higher (at $199 per case).[13] Thus the two counties with the state's most severe concentrations of poverty and highest cost of living receive just 84 percent (Hennepin) and 101 percent (Ramsey) of the statewide average for the two funding streams combined.

Sanctions

The second factor of concern in the early implementation of TANF is sanctions. The initial step for all welfare recipients was attendance at a mandatory one-hour workshop on the new system. The second stage is a meeting with a job counselor to develop an employment, training, or job search plan. In March 1988, nearly 1,000 households of a statewide total of about 48,000 were sanctioned for failing to attend the orientation workshop. Of these families, 783 lost 10 percent of their stipend, and 173 lost 30 percent.[14] Most of these sanctioned families lived outside the state's two most urban counties. Hennepin County, with a caseload of about 16,800, sanctioned only 20 families; Ramsey County, with a caseload of about 10,400, sanctioned only about 150. One month later the statewide sanction rate almost doubled to 1,875. Of these cases, about a fourth (443 families) lost 30 percent of their stipend.

By July 1998, the number of sanctioned households had doubled again to about 3,700, or roughly 8 percent of recipients.[15] Of these, about half were sanctioned at the 10 percent rate and half at 30 percent. The July 1998 county-to-county sanction rates varied dramatically, ranging from 0 to 25 percent of active cases. The wide range does not simply reflect a few outliers. Sanction rates exceeded 11 percent in 24 of 87 counties and were less than 5 percent in 17 counties. The three largest caseload counties (Hennepin, Ramsey, and St. Louis) showed rates near the statewide average, but the relatively uneven enforcement of sanctions in the rest of the state is troubling, even in a state that emphasizes local discretion. It is doubtful, for instance, that this range can be explained solely by differences in caseload compositions.

Work Incentives

An important part of the philosophy of welfare reform is reducing the incentives to enter the welfare system and, similarly, enhancing the incentives to enter private employment. Welfare programs across the country have often been criticized for the high implicit tax rates on workers who leave welfare — the percentage of an increase in private income that is lost to a worker because of increases in taxes or decreases in benefits. Income disregards may be structured in ways that tax away large percentages of increases in private income through reductions in stipends and eligibility rules for other benefits such as childcare support or health insurance may create income "cliffs" when clients leave welfare. Benefit structures for welfare may also interact with other public subsidies, copayment schedules or the tax system in ways that create high implicit tax rates for some income ranges.

The MFIP demonstration reduced the implicit tax rate on non-welfare income from 70 percent (the AFDC rate) to 61 percent. Although this is a significant cut, the MFIP rate still represented a significant reduction in the incentive for people to work. The new TANF rate of 64 percent, although an improvement over AFDC, is similarly severe. As in most parts of the country, there is little or no political support in Minnesota for significant cuts in the implicit tax rate, because such a policy would increase the income at which clients still receive a stipend and raise the cost of the program. This means the primary incentives for work must be coercive, in the form of mandatory participation requirements and the five-year limit.

Minnesota has attempted to ease the transition off welfare by making benefits like childcare and heath insurance available to working poor families. However, the sliding-scale childcare program is not fully funded for non-welfare households, creating an incentive for participants to enter the welfare system to "jump the queue." And transitional services end after one year in most cases, delaying but not eliminating the cliff effect for welfare participants.

Finally, even when welfare benefit schedules are amended to reduce the implicit tax rate on outside income, declines in other public subsidies may offset such changes. Overall, simulations by Minnesota DHS that compute the income available to Minnesota families at various earned-income levels, after accounting for welfare stipends, state and federal tax credits, childcare subsidies and copayments, and several other smaller public subsidies show a very erratic pattern of work incentives. At earned incomes up to those represented by full-time work at the minimum wage, implicit tax rates are modest (20 to 25 percent). However, welfare recipients working full time and earning between the minimum wage (or roughly $10,700 per year) and $6.50 per hour ($13,520 per year) confront an implicit tax rate that exceeds 80 percent. Thus the total support system does well at rewarding the decision to work, but poorly at rewarding additional effort or training that increases wages from very low levels.[16] This illustrates a longstanding problem with the American patchwork quilt approach to income policy: Individual programs, each of which may look reasonable, can interact to undermine incentives for individuals to work more or pursue higher-paying positions.

The Economy

Officials in the Twin Cities metropolitan area have also echoed the concern voiced by Mayors Ed Rendell and Rudy Giuliani in

Philadelphia and New York that, over the medium and long term, local economies are unlikely to absorb all the welfare recipients that the new law pushes into the job market. In Minnesota, unemployment rates have posted historic lows through the first year of welfare reform, and welfare caseloads have continued to decline. (The statewide average monthly caseload dropped from more than 64,000 in 1994 to about 49,000 in 1998.)[17] However, nobody expects the current economic expansion to continue indefinitely. When the economy slows, and when large numbers of families begin to reach the five-year benefit limit, the system will inevitably face problems matching welfare clients with private-sector jobs.

Initiatives intended to address this issue began to surface immediately after passage of Minnesota's TANF bill. The most prominent, approved by the Minneapolis City Council, sets aside for welfare recipients 20 entry-level jobs per year — about 20 percent of the annual entry-level positions posted by the city and the local school district. About half of the recipients would go directly into regular jobs, one-quarter would participate in on-the-job training for two to six months, and a quarter (the hardest to employ) would work in positions supplemented by intensive counseling for three to six months. Although this kind of response is admirable, it is also inadequate, measured against the roughly 16,800 welfare cases on the rolls in late 1998 in Hennepin County. It remains to be seen if similar initiatives will be forthcoming, and if they will put a serious dent in the numbers of recipients eventually forced off welfare by the new time limits.

Program Evaluation

It is still too early to determine how all these concerns will affect the TANF reforms. Minnesota has a good reputation in program evaluation, and at least three studies are under way. The Manpower Demonstration Research Corporation is scheduled to release a second evaluation of the MFIP demonstration that will examine outcomes for up to three years. The Minnesota Department of Human Services is also tracking 2,000 cases over time. Finally, the Minnesota legislative auditor is in the midst of a one-year program evaluation that will document the varying strategies pursued by the state's 87 counties. In 12 to 18 months, the state should therefore be better able to determine how its welfare programs are working.

Conclusions

The initial legal and political transition from AFDC to TANF went relatively smoothly in Minnesota. Administrators were well-prepared for the transition and had a tested template in place. The Democratic legislature and the Republican governor were on the same page, for the most part, in developing of the legislation, and the final bill enjoyed broad bipartisan support. The state's economy was in the midst of a long expansion, consistently outperforming the national economy and exhibiting all-time record low unemployment.

However, even in this relatively ideal environment, the viability of Minnesota's welfare program can be questioned. A rigorous evaluation of the demonstration project used as the template for the new program showed that it performed better than the old AFDC program only for particular segments of the target population, and at relatively high cost. TANF is a watered-down version of the demonstration, with much less education and training available to participants, and the financial incentives to work are also weaker. It is reasonable to expect the program's outcomes to reflect these differences. Even in its watered-down form, the strategy is a potentially expensive one that could eventually outstrip the state's political will to finance it, particularly if the economy slows down and caseloads rise. It is also unclear whether the state's private economy can absorb enough welfare recipients over the long run. Finally, early indicators such as a ballooning sanction rate suggest that the program is not yet reaching all the recipients that it needs to for success.

References

Collins, Barbara J., Shawn Fremstad, and Bruce Steuernagel. 1998. *The Employment and Training Component of Statewide MFIP: An Early Report on Initial Implementation Trends and County Service Delivery Variation*. St. Paul: Legal Services Advisory Project.

Hagen, Jan L., and Irene Lurie. 1992. *Implementing JOBS: Initial State Choices*. State University of New York, Albany: The Nelson A. Rockefeller Institute of Government.

Luce, Thomas. 1998. State Capacity Study: Welfare and Related Services. State University of New York, Albany: The Nelson A. Rockefeller Institute of Government.

Luce, Thomas, Mary Kay Olson, and Sheila Ards. 1994. Implementation of the JOBS Program for AFDC Recipients in Minnesota. State University of New York, Albany: The Nelson A. Rockefeller Institute of Government.

Miller, Cynthia, Virginia Knox, Patricia Auspos, Jo Anna Hunter-Manns, and Alan Orenstein. 1997. *Making Welfare Work and Work Pay: Implementation and 19-Month Impacts of the Minnesota Family Investment Program.* New York: Manpower Demonstration Research Corp.

Minnesota Department of Human Services. 1999a. Low-Income Single Parents: Public Assistance Benefits and Earned Income. St. Paul: Department of Human Services.

Minnesota Department of Human Services. 1999b. Report on Family Self-Sufficiency and Medical Programs. St. Paul: Department of Human Services.

Endnotes

1   The income disregard for participants in the MFIP demonstration was $.39 compared with $.30 for AFDC participants. (In other words, MFIP participants lost $.61 of welfare stipend per dollar of private income compared to $.70 per dollar for AFDC recipients.) For many AFDC recipients, the effective disregard was actually less than $.30, approaching zero for some. After MFIP recipients became ineligible for a welfare stipend, they also qualified for an additional 12 months of Medicaid and childcare transitional services, benefits not generally available to AFDC recipients.

2   In anticipation of federal changes, the state had already applied to the Department of Health and Human Services for a waiver to replace its current AFDC system with MFIP.

3   See Luce et al. (1994) and Hagen and Lurie (1992) for more on JOBS and STRIDE.

4   Minnesota has attempted to implement similar policies in the past but, as in other states, they have always been overturned in the courts. This most recent attempt also failed to win approval in the first round of review in the state courts.

5   Minnesota is home to a large number (roughly 60,000) of Hmong immigrants who came to the U.S. after serving as allies in the Vietnam War. The vast majority of these immigrants are legally in the U.S., and large numbers of older Hmong have experienced difficulties in becoming citizens because of language barriers. All these factors were raised in the debate on the subject and mitigated against treating the Hmong harshly in the welfare system.

6   In 1998 only two counties enrolled more than 10 participants in CWEP, and the statewide total for the year was just 154.

7   The 120 and 140 percent cutoffs for TANF and MFIP are averages that do not apply to all family types, or for all assumptions regarding shelter costs and childcare expenses (which affect food stamp benefits).

8   It is worth noting that, at low income levels, the old AFDC regime for participants in months 5 through 12 had one very undesirable characteristic. This is that clients effectively lost 100 percent of any additional private income because of reductions in their welfare stipend. In this range of incomes (from roughly $1 per month through $645), AFDC recipients effectively had no financial incentive to work whatsoever.

9   The discussion of education and training funding is based on Collins et al. (1998), pp. 19-26.

10   The *Minneapolis Star-Tribune*, May 14, 1999, p. B-1.

11   The *Minneapolis Star-Tribune*, April 19, 1999, p. B-1.

12 Collins et al. (1998), Table 4, p. 21.

13 Collins et al. (1998), pp. 76-77.

14 March and April 1998 data are from the *Minneapolis Star-Tribune*, March 5, 1998, p. 1.

15 July 1998 data are from Collins et al. (1998). The reported sanction rates actually understate the incidence of sanctions. The reported figures include all cases in the denominator of the calculation, even though about 13 percent of cases in the state represent families where no parent or caregiver is subject to sanctions.

16 See Minnesota Department of Human Services (1999a). The simulations are for a single-parent family with two children. The calculations also show that the problem does not end when families no longer receive a welfare stipend. At wage rates from $8 ($16,640 per year) to $20 per year ($41,600 per year), the implicit tax rate is roughly 100 percent. Indeed, in some income ranges the cumulative effect of reductions in benefits from individual programs exceeds 100 percent—income after taxes and childcare expenses actually declines as private income increases.

17 Minnesota Department of Human Services (1999b).

Chapter 6

MICHIGAN'S WELFARE REFORM: GENEROUS BUT TOUGH

Carol S. Weissert[1]

Since 1992, Michigan has been a leader in reforming welfare. Led by an ambitious and savvy governor, the state has reshaped its approach to public assistance to emphasize work first, revamped and recast agencies responsible for the program, and devolved responsibility for putting recipients to work to hundreds of nonprofit and for-profit agencies. The numbers are impressive: In FY 1998, the average monthly welfare caseload was 123,392 — down from 229,349 in 1993 (see Figure 6-1). By June 1999, the state's welfare caseload had fallen to 86,100, its lowest level since 1970 (Governor's Office 1999a). What's more, over 35 percent of remaining recipients in December 1998 had earned income, with average monthly earnings totaling $623. In contrast only 16 percent of clients in December 1992 reported earned income, with a monthly average of $396 (Michigan Family Independence Agency 1999).

Like many others around the country, Michigan's program aims to put recipients to work and provides education and training only as a supplemental effort. The state's requirement that women work after each child is three months old and its recently enacted drug-testing and fingerprinting policies are fairly tough. However, unlike other states, Michigan has not adopted any time limits on benefits, it has a generous childcare program that encompasses both

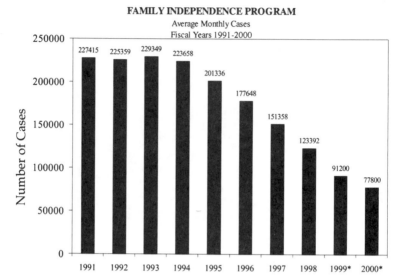

FAMILY INDEPENDENCE PROGRAM
Average Monthly Cases
Fiscal Years 1991-2000

* The caseload figure for fiscal year 1999 is a projection. The FY2000 caseload is from the Executive Budget.

welfare recipients and the working poor, and it facilitates the transition to work through earnings disregards, Medicaid buy-in, and cash instead of food stamps. While considerable political rhetoric has focused on the harshness of the Michigan program, its success may stem from its blend of stringency and compassion — a focus on jobs accompanied by an understanding that barriers must be surmounted to succeed in those jobs. An innovative demonstration project called Project Zero targets those barriers and provides additional political and fiscal resources in a few settings.

The changes in the way Michigan provides welfare assistance involve both organizational reform and a shifting of power — from the welfare agency to the jobs commission and from local welfare offices to a spate of jobs-related agencies across the state. This model reflects the vision of a governor and his top welfare advisor but has evolved into something somewhat different that reflects underlying humane constraints and political realities. The Family Independence Program (FIP), which replaced AFDC in 1996, is much broader than its entitlement predecessor, encompassing cash assistance and job placement and the for-profit and nonprofit sector in the delivery of services in ways not possible under AFDC.

The success of Michigan's welfare reform has tended to over-shadow the political and policy changes that have made it possible. But it is these changes that will persist — long after the media have moved on to other policy areas and political concerns. It is these changes that this chapter will highlight.

The Origins of Michigan's Welfare Reform

Michigan is a highly competitive two-party state that has tradition-ally provided high levels of welfare and unemployment support. State leaders often think of themselves as pioneers in health, wel-fare, and economic development. The state manifests a strong fun-damental support for humane treatment of the poor and needy. As Browne and VerBurg note in their 1995 Michigan political history, "Policy battles are not waged, for example, over questions of whether the state will assist the poor with housing, health care, or fi-nancial assistance. These answers become given.... The moralistic culture assumes that such assistance will be provided to the less for-tunate, although policymakers will debate vigorously the level of support to be given to recipients."

In 1992, Michigan's fledgling Republican governor, John Engler, launched an ambitious program called To Strengthen Mich-igan's Families (TSMF). Inherent in the program was the view that Michigan's families should be bolstered through employment, job training, education, and community services. The goal was keeping families together and enabling them to achieve independence. The proposal contained important provisions regarding earned income and work limitations, but training and education components were also prominent. The initiative called for expanding a program to train and educate AFDC recipients called EDGE (Education De-signed for Gainful Employment), for example. The state obtained a federal waiver in 1992 that introduced a social contract, allowed cli-ents to keep more of their welfare grant while earning income, broadened AFDC eligibility for two-parent families, and allowed AFDC children to earn and save without affecting program bene-fits.

In 1994 the state obtained a second set of waivers that strength-ened the connection between the social contract and the state's fed-erally mandated JOBS program, introduced a new job search requirement, and applied heavier financial sanctions for noncompliance. The new guidelines mandated immunizations for children, allowed deductions for investments supporting self-employment, excluded vehicles when counting clients' resources, and extended some of the AFDC policy changes into the food stamps program.

A Strong Governor Takes the Lead

The Michigan welfare reform story cannot be told without understanding the strong role Governor Engler has played. Shortly after he was elected in November 1990 with one of the state's smallest victory margins, John Engler hinted at his future welfare endeavors, saying, "Our goal should not be to have the best welfare programs but the smallest welfare program in America with the most people at work" (Weissert 1992, p. 155). A few months later he continued this emphasis, saying, "I'm comfortable that the majority of people in Michigan believe that work is desirable over welfare and the incentives should be tilted toward working as opposed to not working" (Weissert 1992, p. 155). Engler maintained that he was committed to caring for the truly needy but that those who could find a job should do so. However, only 10 months into office, Engler and Gerald Miller, the director of the Michigan Department of Social Services, succeeded in eliminating the state's program of general assistance (GA) for unemployed adults. The governor's rationale was that GA recipients were "able-bodied people who should get jobs." However, the GA program was ended partly to help the state through serious financial difficulties in 1991 (Thompson 1995).

In June 1992 Governor Engler called for changing welfare "from a handout to a helping hand, encouraging independence and self-reliance, while building self-esteem. We will succeed by encouraging employment, targeting support, increasing responsibilities, and involving communities" (Gongwer 1992). Some 18 months later, the governor put more emphasis on work first. In February 1994, Governor Engler told the National Press Club in Washington, D.C. that Michigan's plan was based on the idea that "any kind of work in the private sector is better than being trapped on welfare" (Gongwer 1994a).

The governor was unhappy with job-training models such as the state's JOBS program (the Michigan Opportunity and Skills

Training, or MOST). Only 22 percent of those eligible for MOST actually participated in 1994, owing in part to lack of funding for educational programs and support services (Program on Poverty and Social Welfare Policy n.d.). Michigan did not take advantage of the federal moneys available for the program. Several state officials noted that too often MOST graduates could not find jobs in the areas in which they had trained.

In 1994, the governor introduced Work First, which replaced MOST and EDGE and was housed in the newly formed Michigan Jobs Commission (MJC) rather than the Department of Social Services (DSS). While Democratic legislators criticized the Engler administration for putting the poor in "policy traps" with no time to obtain advanced training, DSS Director Miller defended the new approach as the first step to "self-support" (Gongwer 1994b). The governor's press secretary was more direct, saying, "Our system is built on allowing a person to climb his way out of poverty. No longer can they sit back and live off of welfare checks without making an effort to work" (Gongwer 1995a).

The shift in emphasis from family preservation to work first partly reflected the state's strong economy. As one Michigan Jobs Commission staffer put it, "We moved to a point where there were jobs, so it made sense and makes sense in the current economy to have a program that focuses on immediate labor force attachment."[2] Gerald Miller told audiences that the fact that employers kept coming to him asking for employees drove his support for work-oriented welfare reform.

In December 1995 Michigan became the first state to enact sweeping welfare reform in anticipation of federal legislation. Seven months later Washington produced its major welfare reform overall, but Michigan had laid the groundwork. The timing was important. It was early enough for the state — and its ambitious governor — to claim bragging rights to the state's innovations in this important policy area. It was also early enough to see the state's welfare agenda evolve from the 1992 approach — with its focus on helping individuals overcome barriers — to its new focus on jobs, jobs, jobs.

In a highly unusual move, the 1995 law establishing the new Family Independence Program (FIP) gave a great deal of discretion to the Department of Social Services — now called the Family

Independence Agency (FIA). The legislation contained few directives, and the department was free to develop policies without following Michigan's Administrative Procedures Act (APA). The department sought the exemption to speed up the process while avoiding lawsuits from advocacy groups. There were a few constraints on the agency, however. One provision did require DSS to submit policy changes to both House and Senate committees 30 days before implementing them. Another provision allowed the APA exemption for only one year, rather than the 18 months sought by the DSS. Finally, Michigan's law called for publication of draft rules and regulations and public hearings, and directed state departments to consider public views in hearings when writing the final rules.

The governor and Miller were actively involved in the passage of the 1996 national welfare reform bill and had much at stake in the success of Michigan's program. "If the governor wants to make his national reputation on welfare reform, he can't afford to have it fail," said one interest group leader. Indeed, the governor enjoyed considerable national attention in 1995 and 1996 owing to welfare reform. *The New York Times* dubbed Engler the "conservative hero from the Rust Belt" and the "unlikely face of revolution" (Berke 1995). Reporters arrived from across the country to see for themselves how welfare reform was succeeding (Jeter 1997).

Clearly the governor's national prominence is not unwelcomed, and the governor has not shied away from claiming the state is first, the best, and the leader in state welfare reform. In a January 1998 press release the governor boasted that "Michigan was among the first five states to apply for the additional [federal] funding (Governor's Office 1998a). A year later he said, "No other state can claim eight counties where all welfare recipients are working and earning income" (Governor's Office 1999b). The support for Michigan's success comes primarily from anecdotal evidence — there are very few outside evaluations of the program or its demonstration project called Project Zero. The governor tends to be rather thin-skinned about any results that are not supportive of his success scenario, disputing the lukewarm findings of an early study conducted by Abt Associates (Berke 1995), and questioning the bias of a Tufts University report that ranked Michigan in the middle among all states in progress toward increasing the economic security of poor families (Swavy 1998).

In fact, the governor has so dominated Michigan's welfare reform agenda that few groups or persons argue with the basic premise of his plan — putting welfare recipients to work. The governor is the lead architect, promoter, and overseer of the program. He continues to take a personal interest in the program, and his staff regularly monitors reports and progress.

The Limited Legislative Role

The executive branch played dominant roles in two primary components of Michigan's welfare reform — the federal waivers in 1992 and 1994 that allowed the state to implement TSMF and the 1995 welfare reform law. The DSS drafted the federal waivers and worked with the federal Health Care Financing Administration (HCFA) to develop them into acceptable form. The legislative branch was not consulted. (Legislation introduced in the 1997 session called for consultation on future waivers.)

The December 1995 law was enacted when both houses of the legislature were Republican. The governor unveiled the proposal on October 31, 1995, and signed it into law on December 6th. Legislative debate on this important bill was muted and short. One legislator called the process "a greased railroad," arguing that no effort was made to consider the issues of wages, transportation, and childcare that would truly break the cycle of dependency (Gongwer 1995b).

Democrats complained about the lack of public input. The Michigan House held three public hearings in three days. Fewer than 25 people testified, only 4 of whom were private citizens. The Senate held two hearings and heard testimony from 16 people (Michigan's Children 1997). One senator asked why a Senate subcommittee on yard waste could hold hearings around the state, but a hearing on something as fundamental as changes to the state's welfare system was not possible (Gongwer 1995c). Republicans claimed they put the bill on a fast track because a bill delayed until January would not go into effect until the April of the following year, unless the legislature, with an extraordinary majority vote, specified an earlier start date. Republicans were afraid that the Democrats would refuse to do so.

Clearly the legislature as well as the governor wanted to pass the country's first welfare reform bill. As the House speaker put it, "It [the bill] keeps Michigan as a leader in welfare reform" (Gongwer 1995d). DSS Director Miller, following the final passage of the bill, noted that it was appropriate for Michigan to be the first state to enact a welfare reform package since the governor had taken the lead nationwide (Gongwer 1995d). However, the House minority leader complained that "this so-called reform was presented just last week, and there is no reason, other than John Engler's desire to remain in the national spotlight, that we had to vote on this so quickly" (Gongwer 1995e).

In 1996 the Michigan House of Representatives began to hold hearings and gather information on welfare reform. But its actions were limited. In 1997 the legislature passed no significant welfare legislation. Instead the appropriations committees included directives in the budget bill requiring the state to study the outcomes for recipients who participated in Work First, to develop and implement policies in compliance with the domestic violence provisions in the federal law, and to notify recipients of the availability of transitional childcare, including instructions on obtaining a childcare application. In subsequent years, the legislature has added more requirements for reporting, and in 1999 directed the state jobs agency to allow education and training to apply toward work participation requirements.

Interest Groups and Other Actors

Interest groups were not involved in the welfare reform plan prior to the 1992 launching of TSMF but played a more active part in the planning process before the major federal and state welfare reforms. In fact, the planning process was unusually inclusive — involving thousands of Michigan residents in focus groups across the state. DSS formed external advisory groups in four areas: cash assistance, childcare, child protection, and Medicaid. Advisory groups were composed of 50-100 people who were asked to return to their communities and conduct focus groups in which over 4,000 people participated in late 1994 and early 1995. Internal work groups in DSS, co-chaired by central office staff and county directors, reviewed current policies and considered recommendations from the advisory groups.

The process of "fanning out" and using focus groups was new to the DSS. The DSS director and the Medicaid director spoke often of this effort with great pride. One interest group leader felt generally that DSS did listen to the groups, but others were more skeptical. "The governor's office already knew what they wanted and pretty much stuck with their plan regardless of what the focus groups had to say," one advocate said. "The focus groups were more of a cover than having real input in policy."

Interest groups have long been concerned about the long-term viability of the work-first notion in Michigan. These groups include the Michigan League for Human Services, an advocacy and research group representing nonprofit groups across the state that provide social services and citizens concerned with human service issues; Michigan's Children, a state association of children's advocates linked to the National Association of Child Advocates; the Hunger Action Coalition, a nonprofit interfaith, anti-hunger organization based in Detroit; and the Michigan County Social Services Association, which represents county directors, deputy directors, and members of FIA advisory boards. Of particular concern to these groups is the impact on newly hired welfare recipients when the state goes into one of its periodic recessions. Several groups have called for increased focus on educational and training programs to provide these workers with long-term skills. Other issues of concern include staffing in local FIA offices, the size of the assistance grant, and the amount of earned income disregarded before assistance levels are calculated (MLHS 1997).

Some interest groups also worry that too much attention is focused on welfare caseloads while caseloads for childcare and Medicaid are rising. The Michigan Assemblies Project (1998), which held meetings around the state in 1997, has called for increasing education and skill-enhancing opportunities, developing an adequate job base, and enhancing public transportation. Labor has not been actively involved, although most people think that the state's reluctance to rely on community service stems from labor unions' concerns. With the state's robust economy, the community service option is moribund.

The local governmental role in welfare reform in Michigan is minimal. The state's county association has no position on welfare reform and is not closely following the issue. At the local level, the county role is limited to appointing two members to county social services boards that oversee the local FIA offices. Most counties do not contribute funds for welfare programs. There is more local involvement on the work-first components of the state's welfare program. Local officials name members of the workforce development commissions that oversee the job-related activities of welfare reform at the local level (from lists submitted by local chambers of commerce).

Michigan foundations have played a supportive role in implementing welfare reform by funding studies and education. For example, the Community Foundation for Southeastern Michigan has funded childcare centers, learning centers to help move families into self-sufficiency, and a program to teach low-income families financial planning. The Council of Michigan Foundations supported the efforts of a researcher to delineate the community challenges to building welfare-to-work programs and widely distributed the report. The McGregor Fund in Detroit has supported organizations aimed at improving job-training programs for former welfare recipients, and at helping teenage mothers live with their parents or other responsible adults (Skillman 1998).

Program Design

Michigan's welfare system has traditionally been state centralized, with county offices staffed by state welfare department employees. The state's jobs program has been more decentralized, with funding flowing to local workforce development boards. The two approaches could not be more different.

Michigan's Family Independence Program (FIP) has grafted the two programs together, giving welfare offices responsibility for determining eligibility and providing some support services, and workforce development boards the responsibility for providing job training and employment opportunities. The two organizations must work together in Lansing and in the state's 83 counties

Before being signed up for FIP, clients must attend an orientation session jointly sponsored by the FIA and the local workforce development agency called Michigan Works! Clients must then meet with a Work First counselor for an individual orientation. After orientation, the clients must complete a personal responsibility plan and family contract that specifies the family's and agency's responsibilities and plans for meeting the goal of self-sufficiency. The plan assumes that clients will find unsubsidized work, either on their own or with the assistance of Work First counselors.

Some 37 percent of the FIP caseload (33,000 cases in January 1999) is deferred from the Work First requirements. Over 60 percent of these deferrals are children receiving assistance who are being cared for by relatives whose income or assets make them ineligible. Of the remaining, nearly half are deferred because of incapacity or disability and one-quarter because they are mothers of children three months of age or younger (MFIA 1999).

To reward people for working, Michigan offers an earnings disregard of $200 and also disregards 20 percent of the remainder when calculating public assistance levels. This means that a family of three obtains an additional $236 a month by working 20 hours a week at a minimum wage job (MLHS 1997). In September 1992, one month before the implementation of TSMF, some 16 percent of Michigan's AFDC cases reported earned income. By January 1996, that proportion had risen to 31 percent (Miller 1996). Two years later the total reached 35 percent (MFIA 1999).

Job Training

The 25 Michigan Works! agencies (MWAs), responsible for the job search and job readiness portion of Michigan's welfare reform system, also administer a number of federal and state programs designed to prepare youth and unskilled adults for entry into the labor force. The MWAs originally could provide the FIP training themselves, but as of October 1997 they must contract out this work to profit or non-profit agencies called Work First agencies. These agencies help clients locate job opportunities and increase their chances of being hired and successful in those jobs. In some cases this involves language classes; in others it might entail assistance with resume writing or interviewing skills. The agencies must meet specified performance standards and provide regular reports to the MWAs on the number of clients and closed cases, average wage at placement, clients' employment rates, and cost per enrollee. Originally, the agencies were required to report on clients' job situations only at 90 days; the state now requires reporting at three months, one year, and three years after initial placement. About one-fifth of the Work First providers are paid according to their success at meeting performance outcomes; the majority are reimbursed for actual costs (Seefeldt, Danziger, and Anderson 1999).

Work First agencies develop individual service plans to move participants into any type of unsubsidized employment as quickly as possible and increase the responsibility and amount of work the participant is able to handle over time. In the early years of the program, post-employment training or occupational training up to one year in duration was available only to clients meeting the minimum participation requirements of at least 25 hours a week of work. However, in fall 1999, at the urging of the legislature, the state adopted new policies liberalizing the education and training component so that FIP recipients working 10 hours a week and enrolled in education programs for 10 hours can meet the state's 30-hour work requirement (which count 10 hours of study time). The program is limited to one year. Similarly a 30-hour-a-week vocational education program can now also substitute for work for six months.

Dovetailing with these efforts is the governor's No Wrong Door 1997 initiative, which gives clients easy access to other federal and federal-state training programs, including the Job Training Partnership Act (JTPA), summer youth programs, school-to-work, and employment services.

Childcare, Child Support, and Teen Pregnancy Prevention

Michigan's FIP pays 100 percent of current clients' childcare costs; low-income residents not on FIP pay a sliding scale fee to participate. Michigan provides funding for families at or below 60 percent of the median income, with a state match of from 30 to 90 percent varying by income level and family size. There is no time limit for daycare assistance, as long as the person has a low enough income to qualify. Payments are made directly to daycare centers, family daycare homes, and group daycare homes, which must be licensed to receive payment. The state will also pay for daycare aides and relatives who provide care, but they must be enrolled by FIA.

As a result of this rather generous policy, the state's daycare caseload has skyrocketed. In 1991, the caseload was 14,000; by 1998 it had reached nearly 57,000 (MFIA 1999). Spending for daycare increased by 400 percent between 1992 and 1998 (Governor's Office

1998b). In the FY 2000 budget, the legislature appropriated $614 million — more than an 85 percent increase over the FY 1998 level.

Michigan has also implemented several major initiatives to shore up child support, including requiring employers to report their newly hired individuals to the state, denying or revoking professional licenses as a penalty for nonpayment of child support, and suspending drivers' licenses as a sanction. Despite these efforts, while the state's child support collections increased significantly between 1987 and 1996, the portion of the collections attributable to AFDC/FIP clients actually declined during that period — from 24 to 16 percent (MFIA 1997a).

Although Michigan received $43 million in federal Welfare to Work (WtW) funding in January 1998, it decided to drop out of the program later in the year because of restrictions on the grant. The state had hoped to use the WtW money for a statewide program targeting unemployed noncustodial parents whose child support payments are in arrears and whose dependents are receiving TANF. The state is now using TANF, not WtW, dollars for the program.[3]

The state has struggled with efforts to computerize its child support system to meet federal requirements. The state is one of nine states subject to federal penalty ($4.2 million in October 1998) because of its failure to computerize its child support records in a statewide computer system (Durbin 1999). State officials continue to negotiate with their federal counterparts over the computer system tracking nonpayment. Part of the problem is that the state's child support administration is in the hands of two local groups: county prosecuting attorneys and Friends of the Court (FOCs) — 64 independent bodies responsible for enforcing, reviewing, and modifying child support orders. FOCs operate their own computer systems, and the state has had difficulty convincing them to abandon those systems to join a state effort.

To reduce the pregnancy rate among adolescents ages 15 to 19 from the 1996 rate of 77 per 1,000 to 63 per 1,000, the state sponsors family-planning services, sex education, and abstinence programs in selected communities. It plans to conduct a program designed to inform law enforcement officials, educators, counselors, parents, and young males about the problem of statutory rape. The state has spent more than $3 million per year since 1993 promoting abstinence among 9 to 14 years-olds.

Other Welfare Support Programs

As part of its reform efforts, Michigan has established a Medicaid buy-in program for Project Zero clients whose FIP transition period has ended but who want to continue their Medicaid health care coverage by paying a monthly premium. The state also allows food stamp recipients who earn at least $350 for three consecutive months to receive cash instead of food stamps. Nearly a fourth of food stamp households participated in this program in December 1998 (MFIA 1999). The state announced a pilot rental assistance program in 1999 as a cooperative effort between the Michigan State Housing Development Authority and the FIA. Three Project Zero sites provide temporary rental assistance to families who need to relocate for employment or to be nearer to transportation or childcare in order to obtain or retain a job. The maximum subsidy per family is $200 a month (Gongwer 1999a).

Statewide task forces have focused on transportation, a major barrier for many program clients, but efforts to address this problem have largely been delegated to local offices. Some $2 million of the Michigan Department of Transportation FY 1998 funding was targeted as Work First funding and distributed to the 25 MWAs. In 1999, the state tried a different approach, providing some $1 million in federal grant money to fund 10 bus transit projects in 16 rural counties targeted to help welfare recipients and other low income workers get to and from work. FIP clients can receive a one-time $600 grant for buying a car, $600 annually for car repairs if they are employed, and 15 cents a mile for job readiness and search activities after a job is located but before the first paycheck is received. The state plans to put in place additional assistance for those who with limited help might be diverted from welfare in 2000.

Sanctions

Prior to April 1997, families that did not participate in work-first requirements lost 25 percent of their FIP and food stamp grants. After a year of continued noncompliance the state closed the case. This policy changed in April 1997; new cases can close after 60 days if welfare parents fail to participate in work-related activities. Noncompliance now results in a 25 percent reduction in the grant for four months, followed by case closure. A case must remain closed for a minimum of

30 days before the client can reapply. Families cannot be sanctioned when the parent cannot meet work requirements because childcare or transportation is not reasonably available.

There are also non-employment-related sanctions. Failure to cooperate with efforts to establish paternity and pursue child support for dependent children without good cause results in a grant reduction for up to four months and ineligibility after four months. The state also deducts $25 per month from a family's payment for failure to have one or more children under age six immunized according to schedule.

The number of sanctioned families has grown dramatically over the past few years. Between FY 1997 and 1998, for example, the number of cases closed as a result of employment-related sanctions nearly doubled — from 1,216 to 4,765 (Michigan Family Independence Agency 1999). Some 44 percent of these sanctions stemmed from failure to participate in employment-related activities during the first 60 days. While the increase is significant, sanctions applied to less than 3.7 percent of the total December 1998 caseload.

Sanction rates do vary somewhat among FIA offices, but they send a similar signal to clients. One FIA director noted that before welfare reform, sanctions were so light that some recipients were "thumbing their noses at the system." Another noted that the tougher sanctions sent a message to clients that the FIA was serious in terms of work requirements (Putnam 1998a).

Project Zero

One of the most touted aspects of Michigan's welfare reform effort is Project Zero, under which local offices receive extra resources and flexibility to help clients surmount barriers that prevent them from finding and keeping jobs. Project Zero, announced in Governor Engler's 1996 state of the state message, has attracted the attention of national and even international media. The idea is simple: A few offices seek to reduce to zero the number of families without earned income. The legislature appropriated $2 million in additional resources for the six initial Project Zero sites, primarily for childcare and transportation. The office director of one site explained that it was "left up to them" to reduce the number of unemployed clients in the district.

Project Zero also focuses on collaboration with community providers. Offices are encouraged to work with service organizations and religious groups to provide mentoring, counseling, transportation, and childcare. Several sites have relied on volunteers as well. One Project Zero site featured community members who provided free haircuts, transportation to job interviews, and childcare.

In the summer of 1997, one of the six sites, Ottawa County, announced that its entire eligible FIP caseload was earning some income, and the governor traveled there to note the event. The state added six more sites in the summer of 1997 and appropriated $5 million for Project Zero in the 1997-98 budget. In October 1998 Project Zero expanded to 35 sites, and the FY 2000 budget provides an additional $3 million to expand the program to even more sites.

The governor has given Project Zero great visibility, calling it "perhaps *the* major welfare reform initiative in the United States now" (Michigan Family Independence Agency 1997b). Press releases highlight caseload reductions, and the governor's office reports the number of Project Zero clients reporting income every month. When one monthly report revealed that the number of unemployed Project Zero clients actually grew, a governor's staff member called each of the sites, which had to submit a written report explaining the unexpected increase.

By August 1999, 18 Project Zero sites had at one time seen all of their targeted populations — those without deferments with cases open more than 60 days — working. One county maintained its zero status for more than a month. The governor continues to tout the program, claiming in January 1999 that "Project Zero continues to meet goals no other state can match" (Governor's Office 1999b). "Project Zero is succeeding everywhere and performing like no one thought possible," the governor said in August 1999 on the announcement of the 18th site reaching its goal of having all targeted cases employed for at least one day (Gongwer 1999b).

Second-Order Devolution

Second-order devolution to local governments has been hampered by the state-centered administration of Michigan's welfare program, but joint operation by the welfare agency and the jobs commission has diluted that state centrality somewhat. In fact,

Michigan's second-order devolution is mostly directed to 25 Michigan Works! Agencies and to the small, local nonprofit agencies and organizations that provide everything from job readiness to transportation, from language courses to mentoring programs.

The use of the Michigan Works! agencies for such a major component of Michigan's welfare reform is a substantial change from the more centralized welfare model prior to 1994. With very little state direction, most of the $100 million-plus in federal TANF dollars directed to MWAs can be used for services they feel are important to their clients. Work First providers are under contract with the Michigan Works! agencies to offer services and meet certain benchmarks for success in placing FIP clients. They do not follow similar procedures or models; they are judged only on their success — not on the processes they use to achieve them. They also have great discretion in the use of state dollars.

Other devolutionary efforts are occurring in mental health, child welfare efforts, and aging as the state slowly builds up what are known as multi-purpose collaborative bodies (MPCBs) in counties or groups of counties. MPCBs are composed of local human service providers and consumers, who share planning and implementation responsibilities. Although these MPCBs often have little discretionary authority and few funds, they may well emerge in work-first and other arenas as collaborators.

Implementation Issues

Coordination Between State Agencies

Michigan's welfare reform effort is a joint one between the Family Independence Agency (FIA) and the Michigan Jobs Commission (MJC). The two agencies have very different operating styles and organizational cultures. The FIA — a traditional welfare agency with many more employees than the upstart MJC — tends to be hierarchical, rule-bound, and state-dominated. The FIA has long provided detailed management-based statistics to enable the legislature and others to monitor their progress. FIA offices across the state are staffed by state employees who implement policies uniformly.

In contrast to the local FIA offices, which work closely with Lansing and apply rules and regulations across the state, the MJC system encourages variation and provides few guidelines and little oversight. The MJC operates on a modified business model. The agency's director is referred to as the chief executive officer, the staff in Lansing is kept small, and the work of the agency is conducted not by state employees but by workforce development boards, which administer school-to-work programs, summer youth employment and training and programs under the Job Training Partnership Act (JTPA), along with Work First. The MJC staff for the Work First program include only five professionals and a secretary, and their oversight of the program is largely limited to identifying common problems and possible solutions through site visits and regular meetings with contractors and staff.

Funding for the Michigan Jobs Commission has grown while funding for FIA has declined. In FY 1995-96, FIA's total funding exceeded $7 billion; in FY 2000 it is expected to be only $3.5 billion (MSFA 1999). Caseloads dropped from an average of 226,863 per month in 1994 to 123,392 in FY 1998. In contrast, MJC's Work First funding grew by 24 percent — from $75 million to $93 million in just one year between FY 1997 and 1998 (MHFA 1997).

Many in Lansing feel that the Jobs Commission is the governor's "fair-haired child." Even the legislature seems to treat the Jobs Commission in a special way. Several observers have noted that the appropriations hearings for the two agencies are a sharp study in contrasts. For the FIA, the legislature demands the highest accountability, with numbers on many dimensions and elements. The Jobs Commission has not been held so strictly accountable and relied on more aggregate and limited reporting. However, the legislature is now beginning to hold the agency more responsible, calling for several detailed quarterly and annual reports on Work First activities and progress in helping clients find and retain jobs.

While Gerald Miller was the director of DSS/FIA, he maintained a strong relationship with the governor and had a great deal of personal credibility with state legislators. After Miller's agency lost control of the state's Medicaid program to the state community health department, Miller left the state. His departure in October 1996 was very important given his role as the point person for welfare reform. The directorship was vacant for five months at the very time when Michigan was beginning to deal with the federal law and to implement major changes in the accompanying personnel and information systems. Some thought that the governor had lost interest in the FIA and might dismantle it entirely so it was a relief for many when Marva Hammons came on board in the spring of 1997. Although she took several months to grasp some of the key issues in the Michigan system, informants feel that she soon had a handle on her job and provided a steady hand for the reforms under way. In early 1999 Ms. Hammons left the state and another director, the former welfare director in Iowa, Doug Howard, took the position.

Few overt conflicts have occurred between the welfare and jobs staffs in Lansing, but the policy marriage has had its share of difficulties. As one FIA leader put it, "We had a real learning curve. It has been difficult both at the state and local levels. It took a couple of years before we could work together to implement and coordinate policy."

In Lansing, MJC and FIA staff meet regularly to discuss problems and solutions and also attend Work First forums put on by the Michigan Works! agencies. These forums are intended to be "best practice" sessions that also include policy updates and clarification. MJC and FIA staff also work together on interagency task forces such as transportation and out-of-wedlock pregnancies. The agencies try to coordinate the substance and timing of regulations in areas that cross the two agencies' jurisdiction, such as those governing emergency assistance and work-training requirements.

The two agencies did not collaborate particularly well on a 1996-97 special on-the-job-training (OJT) component funded by $6 million in federal TANF dollars. When the FIA transferred the funds to MJC, the former stipulated that MJC could reimburse an employer up to only $450 per month to cover 50 percent of training costs for non-entry-level positions. As most participants enroll in entry-level training, few benefited from the program.

In addition to changes forced by joint responsibility with the MJC, the FIA has undergone enormous changes in its organizational culture and the responsibilities of its employees. FIA workers ask not only "How can we get this person a job?" but also "Why can't this person get a job, and what kind of help will it take to move this person into the workforce?" One high-ranking FIA official points with pride to the way that the FIA has provided a new vision and focus for the agency. She said, "We have changed the whole direction of social services in Michigan and changed the meaning of social service."

In January 1999 the governor issued Executive Order 1999-1 which split the Michigan Jobs Commission into two entities: a new Department of Career Development (DCD), and a new Michigan Economic Development Corp. The Work First program will remain with the DCD. The new department is dominated by federal programs, including TANF, and will receive only $21 million of its $516 million proposed FY 2000-01 budget from state general funds.

New FIS Workers

In 1997, every FIA office changed its personnel classification and responsibilities to a case manager model for FIP recipients. The newly formed family independence specialists (called FIS) are in charge of assessing clients' needs and serve as brokers for services. Each family has one FIS who helps it develop family independence plans and fulfill them, in part through counseling and home calls. Other workers are classified as eligibility specialists (ES) who handle all state disability, Medicaid, Supplemental Security Income, and non-FIP food stamp cases. Supervisors are known as family independence managers, or FIMs.

For many sites, the change in job content has proven profound. Some offices saw considerable competition for the FIS positions, which have higher salaries and lower case loads than the ES positions. The new jobs required considerable training. Former assistance payment workers did not have experience in the services arena; former service workers were unfamiliar with the innumerable rules associated with eligibility. All were unfamiliar with the strength-based, solution-focused approaches felt to be key to implementing the case-management system. The first few months brought considerable confusion, and a backlog of child welfare cases built up. FIA soon reported that the backlog was alleviated, and that the new system was in place and working well.

Personnel problems were compounded by an early retirement incentive program launched in the summer of 1997 to reduce the size of state government. Over 1,600 FIA employees took advantage of the program (Luke 1997) — around 12 percent of the FIA workforce. MJC, a newer agency with a younger, less-experienced staff, had fewer early retirements. The early retirement system hit shortly after the launching of the new FIS/ES personnel system in April 1997 and caused confusion and additional backup of claims, especially in the childcare arena. The second year continued to bring changes in local offices as some workers found the workload was too demanding and switched to ES status — a process so common it had its own new verb — "deFISing."

Local Cooperation and Collaboration

At the local level, the FIA staff work most closely with the Work First staff contractors who perform the day-to-day job-related work with clients. Here too there is often a clash of cultures. A University of Michigan study of FIA and Work First managers documented the differences in the approaches of the two agencies (Seefeldt, Sandfort, and Danzinger 1998). When presented with a hypothetical case of a single mother with limited work experience, the FIA workers' responses were similar across the state. However, in the decentralized Work First agencies, the services that employees would have provided varied enormously. Some Work First providers wanted to offer classroom training before a job search, lasting from two days to more than two weeks. Others encouraged job search and training at the same time; still others encouraged immediate job search either without preparation or with preparation after the search.

Other difficulties arise because of communication barriers. For example, in one Project Zero site, the Work First contractor was not allowed to talk to case workers — only with the FIA liaison. The contractor found this situation difficult because it encouraged clients to play the caseworker off against the contractor. The contractor has recently been allowed to communicate directly with the caseworkers and the system is viewed as more effective.

Not surprisingly, collaboration between the Work First and FIA staffs is often difficult or non-existent. A University of Michigan survey found that nearly 30 percent of Work First managers said their organization had virtually no communication with their FIA counterparts. Another 38 percent reported little front-line communication with FIA (Seefeldt, Sandfort, and Danziger 1998). This is startling given the shared responsibility for the program. Some problems arise because FIA contact with recipients — once extensive — is now shared with Work First contractors.

Two-Parent Families

Michigan's relative past generosity, and its 1992 reforms using earnings disregards to encourage families to stay together, produced a high population of two-parent welfare families. It was clear after the passage of the 1996 federal law that Michigan was going to have a difficult time meeting the requirement that 75 percent of two-parent families work at least 35 hours a week, so the state has focused on this group. The FIA requires weekly monitoring of two-parent families to see if they are in compliance. Their files often receive special attention from the Work First contractor, and the Michigan Jobs Commission provided special supplemental payments totaling $13.3 million to Michigan Works! agencies in early 1997 for this group. An additional $18 million was appropriated to MJC in FY 1997-98 to increase participation rates of two-parent families to meet federal requirements. As one MJC official put it, "Very few communications go out of here that don't reference the need, the urgency, to meet the two-parent requirement."

In 1995, over 20,000 two-parent families composed 12.4 percent of the FIP caseload. By 1997, the two-parent caseload had fallen to 9,000, or 6.4 percent. The sharp reduction was due partly to efforts to ensure that all two-parent families were correctly coded, with families with one disabled parent redefined. In 1998, Michigan reported that a total of 64 percent of two-parent households were working at least 35 hours a week, meeting the 60 percent adjusted target (MFIA 1999).

Information Systems

In March 1997 the FIA named a new chief information officer and charged her to oversee all of the agency's major automation efforts, including the Child Support Enforcement System (CSES), Services Workers Support System (SWSS), Automated Social Services Information System (ASSIST), and the Electronic Benefits Transfer Project (EBT). Before that, these information systems had been isolated projects with no coordination.

The primary welfare system is ASSIST, which should provide a comprehensive vehicle for registering clients and reviewing their eligibility and services. Although it was supposed to go online statewide in April 1997, the first phase (registration) did not go into effect until August 1998 — to a hue and cry of complaints. Offices reported that clients were backed up in FIA offices waiting for the program to operate, benefit checks were mailed to the wrong addresses, and delays in adding information to the files were common. One manager complained that the system has many annoying problems, such as inconsistent and awkward data-entry procedures.

While FIA hopes for a seamless web, the system is far from seamless now. An FIS now registering a client on ASSIST must turn to another computer program to actually open the case. The seamless system will not be in place for several years.

One problem is that the Client Information System (CIS) database long used by FIA offices does not collate information, which must be transferred to another database for statistical use. Another problem is that the FIA and MJC databases are different. In local offices, the CIS information must be reentered into the Michigan Works! information system. One person usually has that responsibility in the FIA office, and she must use one designated computer. What's more, the Michigan Works! system is based on Social Security numbers; the FIA has its own numerical designation.

Time-Limited Time Bomb

There are no time limits under Michigan's welfare reform law. Michigan's governor has pledged that no one will be thrown off welfare at the end of the five-year federally stipulated period. The assumption has been that the state will take over the payments for those still on welfare. But a closer examination of the numbers reveals that the national time limits could mean a substantial state obligation. An FIA analysis found that 47 percent of the FIP caseload had been on assistance for five years or more. Estimates are that as overall caseloads decline, this percentage will increase. When FIA examined the phase-in of the federal time limit, it found that in the first year (2001), only 8.1 percent of recipients will hit the time limit of five years. But the following year, 38.4 percent will have at least five years of experience on the program and thus be ineligible for federal dollars. Under federal law, the state can exempt only 20 percent of recipients from the five-year time limit. The remaining 18 percent who will have exhausted federal eligibility will have to be covered by state dollars (Skillman 1998).

Economic Downturn

Michigan's work-first program is tied closely to the state's galloping economy. The state's unemployment rate averaged less than 4 percent throughout 1998, the lowest since 1970 (Gongwer 1999c). While celebration of the success of Project Zero sites in getting clients to work is in order, some concern can also be raised about those who still remain unemployed. If unemployment rates are low and employers are clamoring for workers, and Project Zero offices have additional resources with which to lift barriers to employment, what can be said for the thousands of recipients still without jobs? What will they do when the job market is once again difficult, and few funds are targeted to reduce work barriers? In a 1998 conference on welfare reform, one Detroit jobs official noted that of nearly 49,000 FIP individuals referred to Work First in Wayne County, only 33 percent entered unsubsidized employment, and a little more than half of those remained on the job for 90 days. She reported that the mean worker in Detroit worked for 29 hours and was paid an initial $5.86 an hour, which increased to $5.91 an hour after three months on the job, or $8,900 a year (Skillman 1998).

The situation is only marginally better for the state as a whole, even in these positive economic times. In 1997, only 62 percent of FIA referrals attended the required orientations, 44 percent attended Work First seminars, 25 percent got a job, and only 11 percent of those initially referred had jobs at the end of 90 days.[4] There would appear to be fairly large numbers of poor who fall through the cracks and who might suffer far more under harsher economic conditions.

Drug Testing and Fingerprinting

In 1999, the Michigan legislature, at the governor's urging, enacted a law calling for mandatory drug testing of all FIP applicants. Ongoing FIP clients will be tested randomly. Those who test positive will be required to enroll in a substance abuse program; refusal will be cause for sanction. The program will be pilot tested in five counties before applying statewide.

Democrats argued that drug testing constituted a stigma for the poor, and that adequate drug treatment programs to enroll those who tested positive did not exist. Republicans countered that the measure would help the children of drug-dependent parents seek treatment. "This isn't punitive," said one Republican legislator. "This is love. If you don't vote for this . . . that's cold indifference to Michigan children" (Guest 1999). The new FIA director supported the effort, saying "Drug testing is a natural progression if we think about the goals of the program," adding that drug abuse takes critical income away from families.

A second measure signed into law in spring 1999 mandates that adults receiving cash assistance and food stamps must obtain a computerized fingerprint to receive benefits. Supporters urged adoption of the bill largely as an anti-fraud effort to prevent people from drawing benefits under more than one name. Politically, there was less controversy surrounding this measure, perhaps because the procedures are relatively unobtrusive and there are no immediate consequences.

Evaluation

One of the first evaluations of Michigan's early TSMF, conducted by Abt Associates, provided mixed support for the program. The study found that TSMF only slightly increased employment and earnings and reduced welfare participation over four years, among families who were on welfare when the program began in October 1992. These recipients saw their average quarterly employment rate rise by 1.3 percentage point and average annual earnings rise by $223. They averaged an annual cut in welfare benefits of $101 and an increase in family income of $118. The results for families certified under the first waiver (October 1992 through September 1994) or under the second waiver (after October 1994) were mixed. The first waiver group saw cuts in welfare participation and benefits without corresponding increases in reported employment or earnings. The second group — recipients assigned after October 1994 — saw an increase in employment but no significant impact on earnings.

Variations across the groups may have been caused by timing of program implementation and changes in program policies (Abt 1997).

The FIA and MJC are collecting data required under federal law but are not sponsoring independent evaluations, even of Project Zero sites. There is little support in the governor's office or the legislature for answering questions that can be answered only through systematic evaluations, said one official, who noted, "They [the governor and the legislature] are happy about what they know and what they can say," he said.

Conclusion

The introduction of To Strengthen Michigan Families in 1992 had as its theme the desire to help move people off welfare through social contracts, a simplified application system, and an emphasis on making employment profitable for families. These goals remain the center-piece of the state's welfare reform efforts seven years later, which clearly emphasized support for work and work-related activities. The governor and the Department of Social Services director were the moving force in refocusing welfare, probably best epitomized by the change in the agency's name and program, the Family Independence Agency and the Family Independence Program. The Michigan Jobs Commission, later changed to the Michigan Department of Career Development, plays an important role in helping TANF recipients find and keep jobs. Difficulties arose between the two state agencies in early years, but overt problems seem to have been resolved.

There are still growing pains at the local level. Nonprofit and for-profit agencies have a major role in helping clients find jobs with little oversight from Lansing. The advantage is an increased ability to meet local needs and a green light for innovative approaches; the disadvantage is possible misuse of funds and equity problems faced by clients who might find a very different array of services offered in one office compared with those of another.

Project Zero, which provides additional resources and support to help lift barriers to employment, and which emphasizes partnerships with nonprofit and for-profit groups, serves as an important demonstration for the state. The apparent success of the sites — even those in traditionally high-unemployment and low-income regions — has led the state to expand the program and, perhaps most importantly, adopt the same emphasis on work in all FIP offices.

While the governor and his press secretary like to emphasize the "toughness" of the state's welfare policies, in fact in many areas Michigan's welfare reform is not so tough. There are no time limits; working families receive relatively generous earned income disregards; the childcare program is well funded and available to the near-poor on a sliding scale without a time limit; and additional state dollars are available for transportation, childcare, and job search. Thus, while the governor talks tough love, he is careful to stay within the state's rather generous political culture. Second, he has used the demonstration approach in several initiatives to learn what works and what needs to be changed. Michigan has also employed this demonstration approach successfully in other areas.

Welfare reform in Michigan is evolving as the program matures, but the same marriage of harshness and generosity that described its early years remains. In 1999, the state dramatically increased its spending for an already generous childcare program and launched an ambitious training program for non-cash recipients (those who receive childcare assistance, Medicaid, or food stamps only). At the same time it initiated new mandatory drug testing and fingerprinting programs. These 1999 "tough love" components, embraced by the governor and supported by the legislature, reflect themes common to the state's seven-year experience with welfare reform. Another distinguishing characteristic is the state's unwillingness to fully evaluate the effects of its programs. While the legislature is now demanding more data on their progress, there are no major evaluations under way using control groups, panel data, or longitudinal analysis to fully test and learn from demonstration programs and test the validity of the state's claims of success.

References

Abt Associates. 1997. *Final Impact Report. The Evaluation of To Strengthen Michigan Families*. Cambridge, MA: Abt Associates Inc.

Browne, William P. and Kenneth VerBurg. 1995. *Michigan Politics and Government: Facing Change in a Complex State*. Lincoln, NE: University of Nebraska Press.

Berke, Richard L. 1995. Conservative Hero from the Rust Belt. *The New York Times*, February 12.

Department of Health and Human Services. 1998. *Temporary Assistance for Needy Families (TANF) Program: First Annual Report to Congress*. Washington D.C.: U.S. DHHS.

Durbin, Dee-Ann. 1999. New Welfare Director Tackles Child Support. *Ann Arbor News*, March 3, B4.

Gongwer News Service. 1992. Engler Seeks Quick Federal Okay for Fundamental Change in Welfare. *Michigan Report*, June 2.

Gongwer News Service. 1994a. Engler: Give States Flexibility to Try Welfare Experiments. *Michigan Report*, February 3.

Gongwer News Service. 1994b. Engler Welfare Reform Criticized for Yanking Education. *Michigan Report*, October 27.

Gongwer News Service. 1995a. Welfare Reform Proposal Being Unveiled Tuesday. *Michigan Report*, October 30.

Gongwer News Service. 1995b. Democrats Want to Slow Down Welfare Hearings. *Michigan Report*, November 1.

Gongwer News Service. 1995c. Senate Opens Debate on Welfare Reform. *Michigan Report*, November 30.

Gongwer News Service. 1995d. House Finishes First Leg of Engler's Welfare Sprint. *Michigan Report*, November 9.

Gongwer News Service. 1995e. Senate Approves Welfare Reform Bills. *Michigan Report*, December 5.

Gongwer News Service. 1999a. Pilot Welfare Program to Provide Rental Assistance. *Michigan Report*, January 11.

Gongwer News Service. 1999b. Tireman Added to List of Successful 'Zero' Sites. *Michigan Report*, August 2.

Gongwer News Service. 1999c. Unemployment Under 4 Percent for '98, Welfare Continues to Fall. *Michigan Report*, January 20.

Governor's Office. 1998a. Governor Engler Announces Plan for New Welfare Money. January 27. http://info.migov.state.mi.us.

Governor's Office. 1998b. Engler Announces Welfare Child Care Grants. February 2. http://info.migov.state.mi.us.

Governor's Office. 1999a. Michigan Welfare Reforms Move Forward. July 27. http://info.migov.state.mi.us.

Governor's Office. 1999b. Governor Announces Leelanau and Benzie Counties Hit Zero. January 28. http://info.migov.state.mi.us.

Guest, Greta. 1999. Drug Testing of Welfare Applicants Passes House. *Ann Arbor News*, February 10, B7.

Jeter, Jon. 1997. One Place Where Welfare Reform Is Succeeding. *Washington Post National Weekly Edition*, October 20, p. 34.

Luke, Peter. 1997. Retirement Plan Is Clumsy Way to Cut Government. *Ann Arbor News*, June 15.

Michigan Assemblies Project. 1998. *Welfare Reform: How Families Are Faring in Michigan's Local Communities*. Detroit: Groundwork for a Just World.

Michigan Family Independence Agency. 1997a. Financial Assistance Overview. Presented to the House Human Services and Children Committee. March 4, 1997.

Michigan Family Independence Agency. 1997b. Project Zero November Report Indicates Progress. *FIA Icon*, January, p. 6.

Michigan Family Independence Agency. 1999. FY 2000 Executive Budget: Grants and Welfare-to-Work Programs. Presented to the Senate Appropriations Subcommittee for the FIA Budget. February.

Michigan House Fiscal Agency. 1997. *Appropriations Summary and Analysis: Interim Report*. September 1997. Lansing, MI: House Fiscal Agency.

Michigan League for Human Service. 1997. *Assessing New State and Federal Welfare Legislation: Three Critical Questions.* Lansing, MI: MLHS.

Michigan's Children. 1997. *Making Change: The Cost to Michigan Children.* Lansing, MI: Michigan's Children.

Michigan Senate Fiscal Agency. 1999. FY99-200. Family Independence Agency Budget Spreadsheet. http://www.state.mi.us/sfa

Miller, Gerald. 1996. Michigan Looks Ahead to Federal Reform. *Public Welfare* 54,2: 10-15.

Program on Poverty and Social Welfare Policy. *Welfare Reform in Michigan.* Ann Arbor, MI: University of Michigan Program on Poverty and Social Welfare Policy.

Putnam, Judy. 1998a. More Kicked Off Welfare. *Ann Arbor News,* November 29, 1998, p. A1.

Putnam, Judy. 1998b. State Welfare Cases Drop Below 100,000 to 1971 Level, *Ann Arbor News,* December 16, p. A1.

Putnam, Judy. 1999. Engler Seeks More State Funding for Child Care, *Ann Arbor News,* February 12, 1999, p. C5.

Seefeldt, Kristin, Jodi Sandfort, and Sandra Danziger. 1998. *Moving Toward a Vision of Family Independence: Local Managers' Views of Michigan's Welfare Reform.* Ann Arbor, MI: University of Michigan Program on Poverty and Social Welfare Policy.

Seefeldt, Kristin, Sandra Danziger, and Nathaniel Anderson. 1999. *What Contractors Have to Say About the Work First Program: Highlights from Interviews with Work First Managers in Michigan.* Ann Arbor, MI: University of Michigan Program on Poverty and Social Welfare Policy.

Skillman Foundation. 1998. *Update 1998: The Status of Welfare Reform/Devolution in Michigan.* Detroit: Skillman Foundation.

Swavy, Joseph. 1998. State's Welfare Criticized. *State News,* February 25, p. 7.

Thompson, Lyke. 1995. The Death of General Assistance in Michigan. In *The Politics of Welfare Reform*, Donald Norris and Lyke Thompson, eds. Thousand Oaks, CA: Sage, 79-108.

Weissert, Carol S. 1992. Michigan: No More Business as Usual with John Engler. In *Governors and Hard Times*, Thad Beyle, ed. Washington D.C.: Congressional Quarterly Press, 151-162.

Endnotes

1   The author wishes to acknowledge the valuable assistance of two MSU graduate students, Philip Kloha and James Durian, who participated in the interviews and data collection effort.

2   Direct quotes where no reference is cited were obtained in interviews conducted by the author.

3   Michigan applied for second-year grants but does not plan to provide the state match required for their use unless Congress makes changes in the original law.

4   Computed from monthly reports from the Michigan Jobs Commission. The data cover the period from October 1, 1996, to August 31, 1997.

7

Concluding Comments: Welfare Reform and Governance

Thomas L. Gais

Midwest states now have more experience with work-based, time-limited welfare systems than any other region of the country. Two changes are particularly evident in this region: First, welfare policies and administrative structures have incorporated new goals, structures, and activities designed to encourage quick entry into the workforce by low-income families. Bipartisan legislative coalitions have created the new emphasis on jobs by assigning greater responsibilities over welfare programs to employment bureaucracies; by expanding services and resources for childcare, employment services, transportation, and other work assistance; and by giving agencies the authority to require a larger proportion of family heads to work and withhold some or all benefits from families who fail to comply with work requirements.

Second, as the tasks and institutions of welfare have changed, so has the distribution of power over welfare policymaking and administration. Midwestern states are devolving greater responsibilities in designing and conducting programs to local governments, contractors, and local offices of state agencies. Some of this decentralization is explicit, as states give local entities expanded roles as part of a strategy to increase local adaptation to diverse circumstances. Yet much of the downward shift in discretion is an implicit consequence of a service-based and interactive approach to changing behavior. Not only do local welfare agencies have a larger repertoire of treatments to choose from in dealing with parents and other caregivers, the decisions about when and what treatments to apply often involve complex judgments and are not easy to regulate. Some of this "second order" devolution is also due to the growing role of labor bureaucracies, which have traditionally been more decentralized than social service agencies.

Transformations of this magnitude spawn a host of social, political, and economic repercussions. Our work at the Rockefeller Institute focuses on the *institutions* of social policy — what those institutions are organized to do and how they have changed. Richard P. Nathan and I have described these changes in a report we completed for the State Capacity Study, *Implementing the Personal Responsibility Act of 1996: A First Look*.[1] In this chapter, I draw on that report as well as the reforms reported in this book to address issues of governance. While the movement toward complex, decentralized, loosely structured welfare systems enables local agencies to respond to local circumstances and encourage work, this shift also raises such questions as: How can legislatures maintain accountability and control? How can leaders and communities assess or even understand the effectiveness of the new welfare systems? And how can states and localities ensure fairness and equity in their dealings with individuals while pursuing the overall goals of welfare reform? Welfare reform and its strong work and anti-dependency goals are not only posing questions about what works in making families financially independent but also about how we can reconcile these new program structures and operations with our democratic institutions.

Political Control and Accountability

A striking feature of devolution has been the salient and often dominant role played by governors and top state executives and the contrasting political weakness of state legislatures. The recent history of devolution has largely been a history of *executive* action. Governors pushed for increasingly ambitious waivers from Medicaid and AFDC requirements in the early 1990s. And as Carol Weissert points out in this book, governors in the Midwest — as in most states within our research sample — were very active in fashioning the new welfare policies, while state legislatures usually made only marginal changes before the legislation was finalized. If anything, the role of state legislatures has declined even further since the reforms were enacted. This is due in part to the popularity of the reforms and their apparent success in moving parents into jobs and reducing caseloads without clear signs of widespread pain. Most legislatures are just not facing strong pressures to make major program changes.

But there may be longer-term reasons for legislative weakness. Although political support for the work-related goals and basic features of state welfare reforms was widespread in most states, legislators were reluctant to tinker with the details of executive proposals. This reluctance may stem from tensions in the public's views about welfare. According to a national survey conducted for the W. K. Kellogg Foundation in late 1998, large majorities of American citizens support "reducing the number of people on welfare," "eliminating fraud and abuse," "saving taxpayers' money," "making sure poor children get the help they need," *and* "lowering the number of people who live in poverty."[2] These are not necessarily incompatible goals, but they do suggest different priorities about where to invest resources and maybe different policy and administrative decisions about sanctions, safety nets, services, procedures, and agency goals. Many governors recognized that the basic idea of a pro-work welfare reform was much more popular than many of its components, and that led some governors — such as Zell Miller in Georgia and Tommy Thompson in Wisconsin — to fashion comprehensive welfare packages in near secrecy and push for their acceptance in their entirety. In Michigan, the legislature granted extraordinary rulemaking powers to the executive to put together the state's welfare reform. And in Missouri, the legislature has refused to reconcile its AFDC-waiver reforms with federal welfare laws, thereby ceding all responsibility for resolving the differences to the executive. There were exceptions — from Rhode Island to California — but the overall pattern was one of state legislators appearing to be only too happy to leave the divisive details of welfare reform to executive action and interpretation.

Yet legislative weakness may have deeper sources. Legislatures, of course, rely on statutes to exert control over how public benefits and sanctions are meted out and applied, but statutes may not be as important as they once were in shaping the interactions between public agencies and low-income families. As federal and state governments transform welfare systems from entitlement to social service programs, the laws necessarily become more of a framework within which program personnel deal with low-income families than strict guidelines for administrative decisions. The chapters in this volume show an expanding range of tools that local administrators and case managers select from when working with families: sanctions of different levels, diversion payments, various work support services, home visits, personal responsibility agreements, referrals to other public or private agencies, case management, and so on. Many of the decisions that welfare personnel make in applying these tools involve some rather fuzzy distinctions: who is employable, who should be exempt from time limits because they are judged to have long-term employment problems, who should be sanctioned and when, what services are needed and appropriate, what stipulations a personal responsibility agreement should contain, or when childcare is not considered available. This shift toward multiple services and program signals designed to change behavior — sometimes delivered in a highly interactive manner — gives administration a greater role in shaping the actual treatments families receive. Washington State both recognized and contributed to this change when it reduced the administrative codes governing welfare agency decisions from 54 pages under AFDC to only 12 pages under the state's TANF program — despite the fact that TANF involves more, not fewer, program activities and decisions.[3] These complex judgments are not always delegated to local agencies and workers; some decisions — such as exemptions from time limits in many states — may involve top state administrators. But wherever the decisions are made, the reforms push power and discretion into the executive branch or its agents and reduce the explanatory power of law with respect to the actual treatments received by individuals and families. In Wisconsin, for example, sanction rates zoomed up as the result of a single communication by a top administrator, even though no laws were changed. Similarly, Weissert suggests that Michigan's laws as implemented are significantly less "tough" than a comparison of its laws with those of other states might suggest. In sum, the new welfare requires judgments about how people are likely to behave and respond and which tools are most effective in specific instances, and these judgments resist codification and give administrators substantial discretion and control.

One implication of the role of administrative judgment is that influence over welfare may flow to persons or institutions with the capacity to focus the system on particular goals or approaches. This is a capacity that governors and top administrators have — buttressed by their powers of contracting for services, formulating budgets, and making appointments — and that most state legislatures do not. The real questions in understanding welfare systems are answered not by examining policies in great detail but by knowing how public bureaucracies or private service providers actually use their choices and toward what ends. Governor Engler's intense personal attention to Project Zero sites encouraged other Michigan offices to maximize the number of families receiving earnings, and the state's high work participation rates of adults on welfare may be the result. Administrators and governors also control many basic decisions about how programs are structured. In Ohio, the administration, not the legislature, determines the outcome of negotiations between the state and counties over their welfare plans and performance criteria.

One feature of the new welfare institutions is the plurality of goals and agency cultures they now encompass. The 1996 Personal Responsibility and Work Opportunity Act has not so much ended older bureaucratic cultures — including the older AFDC emphasis on using extensive documentation and recertification to minimize eligibility errors — as much as it has introduced new pro-work goals to welfare delivery systems.[4] The real story of devolution may not just be the new block grants but rather the diverse ways in which states blend or give different weights to several coexisting orientations, including "work-first" goals, anti-fraud or error-minimization, access to entitlements (such as food stamps and Medicaid), and skill enhancement through training or education (which may be partly funded with welfare block grant funds but which may also be funded by workforce development money). If this is so, power in the new system may go to those — especially governors and their appointees — willing to use their administrative powers and public leadership to establish priorities among these different orientations.[5]

It is too early to know the consequences of this shift in responsibility and control from legislatures to executives. One possibility may be a growing sophistication in developing welfare systems, as the professional expertise often found in executive agencies exerts greater influence over the design of state and local welfare systems. It is also possible that these systems will become more mutable, as governors come and go and change executive priorities and interests. But a more general effect may be a decline in the scope of political interests influencing welfare policy. Governors are no less accountable than legislatures. Yet legislatures are open to many interests that might not be part of the governor's own political coalition — especially now, as divided party control over state governments is more the norm than the exception. Legislative weakness may thus limit opportunities for effective criticism and counterpressures regarding the structure and operation of welfare programs. These limitations may be quite serious as the federal government also plays a much smaller oversight role in welfare policy, and whether the courts will serve as a significant check on administrative decisions is still unclear.

Evaluating the New Welfare

Some of the same reasons that make it harder for legislatures to control the delivery of welfare services also create enormous challenges for evaluation, especially classical approaches to estimating program impacts. The standard model for impact evaluations relies on a control group of individuals or families to estimate what would happen to a target population in the absence of the program. In the best situations, individuals or households are randomly assigned to the control and treatment groups. A significant difference in outcomes between the control group and the families who did receive program benefits — where outcomes may include employment rates, average earnings, out-of-wedlock births, or child well-being — is then viewed as an estimate of the program impact. If the experiment or quasi-experiment is well executed, and if other potential threats to validity can be dismissed, this kind of study is a powerful tool for distinguishing between effective and ineffective programs. In fact, randomized control group studies in the 1980s and early 1990s were important influences in moving welfare reform away from an emphasis on education and training — which was the central thrust of the Family Support Act of 1988 — and toward the current emphasis on work first.[6]

However, aside from AFDC "waiver" evaluations, which are still going on but will eventually end, few states are conducting major impact studies of their welfare reforms. The small number of impact studies is in part a consequence of the new flexibility states have under the 1996 federal block grant. The U.S. Department of Health and Human Services generally required impact evaluations as a condition for granting waivers from AFDC requirements in the early and mid-1990s; and because many states wanted these waivers, impact evaluations were not uncommon. But now that states can put into effect diverse welfare programs without federal waivers, they have fewer incentives to conduct such studies.

Yet even if states wanted impact evaluations, useful studies, which were never easy, are even harder to conduct now. One problem is attribution: the new welfare encompasses so many treatments and decisions, it is difficult to determine what specifically causes program impacts. The interim evaluation of the New Hope program in Milwaukee is a good example. This study — launched in 1994, before federal welfare reform was enacted — examined the impact of a comprehensive program of extensive work support services, generous earnings disregards, work requirements, and income supplements. The evaluations to date have found moderate effects on parental earnings and a variety of child well-being measures, though the effects on child well-being appear only for the boys. The results are intriguing, but the researchers have not been able to attribute the effects to any particular elements of the New Hope initiative, nor have they been able to explain why boys are affected by the program and girls are not.[7]

For policymakers the attribution issue is serious, since states and localities are much more likely to consider adopting one or more components of a successful reform than a single comprehensive package. Minnesota addressed this question in its AFDC-waiver evaluation of the state's Family Independence Program by creating two treatment groups: one that included sanctions and financial work incentives, and one that included financial incentives alone. Researchers found that the combination of sanctions and positive incentives ("carrots and sticks") was more effective than either incentives alone or AFDC (which the control group received). We do not know, however, the effects of sanctions alone, nor do we know whether the joint effects of sanctions and work incentives depend on some other element of the program.[8]

Estimating the effects of specific components of these complicated programs would require either studying many treatment groups or running experiments one program element at a time. The state might, for example, want to assess whether home visits, childcare vouchers, or more generous earnings disregards will produce better outcomes than the state's current policies by assigning families to two groups: one that is subject to the state's general policies, and one that is subject to these policies plus the experimental element (such as home visits). But the problem with this marginal experimentation is its statistical weakness: the probability that the evaluation will not show any effect even if effects exist. The waiver evaluations suggest that even very different programs — such as AFDC and the New Hope initiative — produce only small to moderate effects on earnings, employment, and other outcome measures. Assessing individual components of these programs would be very difficult because of the basic similarity between the experiences of the treatment and control groups.

A more basic problem is that many of the new state and local welfare reforms are not "programs" in the usual sense. Traditional evaluation methods make sense if treatments are well-defined, replicable, and stable interventions. But the logic and structure of many state welfare reforms — especially among the Midwest states — suggest instead a collection of local systems that organize, mobilize, and adapt a changing mixture of programs and community resources around the goals of employment and anti-dependency. Whether and what forms of diversion assistance are attractive to clients, whether welfare systems can and should stress unsubsidized jobs rather than work experience activities, what forms of transportation assistance are most effective, and what kinds of childcare assistance are needed — all of these depend in part on community characteristics, such as the levels of unemployment, the types of industries and jobs, the capacity of the local transportation system, the current supply of childcare centers, and even the tendency of relatives to live close to one another. We found, for example, that in localities with high unemployment, welfare workers may still try to divert families from cash assistance in an effort to minimize time on the five-year clocks. However, welfare workers also realized that in addition to encouraging employment, they needed in these circumstances to maximize clients' access to public benefits that are not time-limited, such as food stamps and Medicaid. Many local welfare offices or job centers are organized to respond to local conditions: they may, for example, work with local employers to develop special and often *ad hoc* opportunities for low-income families. Some of Wisconsin's job centers show particularly strong interactions with the community by relying on both co-location and referrals to draw on a rich variety of local agencies and programs, including charitable organizations, community and technical colleges, private industry councils, local hospitals, and many others. The centers thus become community focal points for reaching and serving low-income families. Job center programs, including W-2, seem to be influenced in turn by the values, resources, and cultural orientations of community institutions.

As the chapter by Charles Adams and Miriam Wilson makes clear, the basic organization of social service delivery systems can vary enormously. Though this local variation is not unexpected in states like Ohio where counties have long had substantial flexibility, their flexibility has grown enormously as counties now have the opportunity to receive their own "block grant" that contains several different funding streams (including food stamps, Medicaid, TANF, state maintenance-of-effort money, and childcare). In the states that did not rely on counties to administer AFDC, local adaptation is still substantial as many states (such as Michigan, Texas, and Florida) rely on local workforce development boards (or, in the case of Florida, boards that look a lot like workforce development boards) to design and administer work-first programs. Such boards have traditionally been much more decentralized than state welfare agencies. In sum, although there was always some local level variation in AFDC programs, the devolved and adaptive character of the new welfare systems seems to be of a different order.

Variation within states and over time in the structure and content of welfare programs poses a measurement challenge for evaluation: it is not a simple matter to say what the program actually is. But to the degree that local welfare systems are dynamic, motivated, and adaptive, the challenge is more fundamental. Welfare programs may be effective or ineffective not because of the particular treatments they deliver to low-income families. What works and what does not may depend on a host of particular circumstances. If treatment effectiveness depends on context, what accounts for variation in effectiveness may not be the treatments themselves but rather the capacity of local agencies to select and adapt those treatments to the needs and resources of local communities and families. This raises the attribution issue to a broader question for social theory. Should we try to attribute variations in program success to the services delivered and rules applied to families and individuals? Can we expect these conclusions to be generalizable to very different communities, local economic structures, and family situations? Or is it actually more reasonable to evaluate the *systems* that make decisions about what interventions are appropriate and under what circumstances? What type of theory is more likely to be robust? A theory of how individuals and families change their work, reproductive, and economic behaviors, and how public interventions can contribute to that change? Or a theory of what makes an organization capable of detecting problems, learning from its efforts, understanding and adapting its processes, and developing innovative responses?[9] Variations in success might be a function not of whether a welfare system is organized around a work-first approach as opposed to one that also emphasizes training and education services, but of whether the system has the capacity to choose between or even blend these and other approaches with intelligence and in light of full understanding of relevant circumstances. This is not just another way of saying that "implementation matters." Implementation usually means putting a "policy" into effect; it typically connotes a transitional process of creating greater "consonance" between laws and bureaucratic behavior.[10] But I am arguing that laws may be just one of many factors that influence, and that should influence, complex administrative systems. Nothing is *finally* implemented; policies may be created and adapted *all the time.*[11]

The question of which theoretical perspective will produce stable and useful results is still an open one, and quite possibly both viewpoints contain some truth. But the ambiguity about the basic conceptual framework for understanding effectiveness in the new welfare programs means that evaluating the new welfare systems is not just more demanding but a different matter altogether than evaluating, for instance, changes in eligibility rules for cash assistance or social services. In fact, the dynamic character of these systems suggests that, just as there is no final implementation, there may be no final evaluation. Evaluation, to make sense under the new circumstances, ought to be continuous or at least recurrent and built into the management process at the level where critical decisions are being made.

That is a tall order, though interestingly, the states seem to be moving toward this approach. Aside from the remaining AFDC waiver studies, program assessments in the post-TANF world consist for the most part of state "leaver studies" that track the employment status of adults after they leave TANF programs.[12] Such studies seem designed to determine whether persons targeted by the program are in acceptable circumstances, even though the standards of what is acceptable are usually subject to debate. Is it satisfactory if 60 percent of all heads of household who leave welfare are employed after one year? Is it acceptable or distressful if 1 percent of such households lose custody of their children within a year after leaving welfare? And what should we make of a discovery if we learn that one-fourth of leavers lack health insurance? Since no real consensus exists concerning an acceptable level of performance, many "half-full, half-empty" debates ensue.

Although that may be a valuable development as little public discussion on these questions existed before the enactment of TANF, many of the studies are plagued by methodological problems. Studies that rely on surveys often suffer from low response rates and generally overestimate employment, while studies that examine administrative data (such as unemployment insurance) generally underestimate employment rates. But the more fundamental problem is that these studies offer no way of estimating the counterfactual. How many leavers would have been employed if they had not received program benefits and services, or if they had participated in the old AFDC program or in some other version of welfare reform? These studies also focus on only part of the population likely to be affected by welfare reforms, and certainly a nonrandom subset of that population. The studies are only beginning to collect information on families who never enrolled in the program despite their being eligible for it, which may be an increasing proportion of poor families; such families might have been steered away from cash assistance by social stigma, program signals, emergency assistance, or employment services at a job center. The studies also tend not to collate outcome data on employment and earnings with policy, administrative, or economic changes that might help explain variations over time. The studies are almost all conducted at the state level; local welfare agencies rarely report information on leavers. But because of the considerable local-level variation *within* state welfare systems, state-level information may be difficult to interpret, especially by local administrators, local advocacy groups, and others who need to know how their local systems are performing.

However weak, incomplete, or hard-to-interpret the leaver studies may be, they nonetheless point in a useful analytical direction. If we cannot estimate the "program" impact on the target population — if that sort of rational approach to policy assessment is less feasible here — then perhaps we should apply another principle: responsible program personnel as well as citizens and policymakers ought to make decisions in light of full and up-to-date information about the scope of the problems the programs are expected to solve and the status of those who are expected to benefit. To be useful in assessing welfare systems in the post-reform world, studies should be done at the local level, they should include information on nonrecipients as well as recipients (such as poverty data on all families in the locality), the data should be collected routinely and consistently over time, and the state or locality should have the capacity to analyze this information and draw informed (though not necessarily definite) conclusions about the relationships between system changes, the economy and society, and the behavior and well-being of families. We are, however, a long way from putting this informational strategy into effect. At the moment, we do not even have good, recent data on the extent of poverty in counties; local-level data on poverty suffer from large errors and several years pass before the data are available.[13]

In sum, the new welfare presents a real challenge to the use of evaluation — and analytical methods more generally — in fashioning and adjusting public policies. Evaluations are unlikely to use experimental or quasi-experimental approaches after the current AFDC waivers lapse. Even if impact evaluations are carried out, it is not at all clear that the results can interpreted as saying anything particular about what works and what does not — or whether good or bad results are attributable to policies or characteristics of the administrative systems. Building systems that regularly or even continuously monitor outcomes, treatments, and problems — especially at the local level — is perhaps more feasible and fitting, but doing so would demand a much greater investment in public information gathering than we have seen thus far.

Rediscovering Procedural Fairness

An important change brought about by the Personal Responsibility Act was the complete elimination of the regulations governing the processes by which AFDC was administered. These regulations were in part a response to legal rights challenges in the early 1970s.[14] By requiring certain written notifications, establishing timeframes, giving clients options regarding which workers they deal with, specifying appropriate forms of verification, and determining who can and cannot assess eligibility, the procedural rules were intended to minimize discriminatory, inconsistent, and even punitive behavior toward individuals by public assistance agencies and workers. But these extensive procedural regulations were often seen as making welfare agencies inflexible and particularly inconvenient for working parents, who were often treated as likely cheats. To encourage a transformation to a stronger work focus, the 1996 Act relied instead on aggregate performance and outcomes data — and financial penalties and rewards attached to those measures — to reorient state welfare programs and hold them accountable.

The shift toward a stronger emphasis on collective goals has been a major effect of the Personal Responsibility Act and state welfare reforms. Nonetheless, as states pay greater attention to performance in these terms, there has been a growing concern over processes, especially their fairness and equity. To some extent, a concern for fair procedures grows directly out of the emphasis on personal responsibility and independence. People may seek services; they may choose not to accept certain benefits; or they may even want to avoid welfare rolls altogether. All of these choices are reasonable in a free society. But to help people make responsible and independent decisions, they should be informed of their options. Declines in food stamp and Medicaid enrollments have prompted some policymakers, advocacy groups, and citizens to ask whether poor families are receiving too little or even false information about their eligibility.[15] Diversion programs and pre-application job search requirements may discourage low-income families from completing eligibility reviews for food stamps, Medicaid, or childcare, though many families with jobs qualify for these programs. And families who leave welfare rolls for low-income jobs may do so without learning about transitional Medicaid and other benefits they remain eligible to receive.

Even within the TANF program, the growing number of services that increasingly constitute "welfare" often means that clients must sometimes contact numerous persons or agencies to get what they are eligible to receive. However, many clients do not make the contacts. Many poor or near-poor working parents, for example, fail to use childcare benefits. That may sometimes be their preference, as parents choose to rely on family or friends to take care of their children. Yet it is also possible that some parents are not informed of their eligibility, and the pattern of informing or not informing parents may have selective effects on certain groups. In Florida, for example, a survey conducted in 1998 found that only 28 percent of the families on welfare rolls had met with a childcare counselor — and that English-speaking parents were twice as likely to meet with a counselor than were Spanish-speaking parents.[16] Procedural fairness also emerge in the case of sanctions. Sanction rates vary considerably not only between states but also within states and over time. Intra-state variance may be due to differences in compliance, but it may also depend on whether parents are forewarned of their work responsibilities. In Arizona, for example, the large number of sanctions imposed in the first year of TANF implementation may have grown out of the fact that local welfare offices had not yet changed program signals, nor had they created strong procedural connections with employment offices. At least during these early months, some people may have been sanctioned without ever knowing about their work responsibilities or the services they could have used to find employment.[17]

These issues of informational and procedural fairness indicate that local differences in administrative capacity and operations may be increasingly important to the well-being of families. Administrators should be able to manage their processes and ensure that parents or caregivers are given adequate information, that procedures do not break down, and that discretion is exercised according to appropriate criteria and judgments and not according to discriminatory practices. This policy area may raise issues that have long dominated American education policy, where local institutional capacity is not only important to program outcomes but is also quite varied from one locality to another. Yet it is not easy to monitor the new welfare processes, nor is it a simple matter to assess and compare local capacity. It is, of course, possible to impose new regulations to govern the interactions between service delivery personnel and clients — and to some extent, that is what the federal government is doing to ensure better access to Medicaid and food stamp benefits — but regulations are harder to enforce when so many different public and private agencies are delivering services, and when the interactions between agencies and individuals are so rich, complex, and even messy. Thus, the concerns for equitable treatment are not disappearing even though welfare is no longer a federal entitlement, while the challenge of monitoring procedures and distinguishing between fair and unfair practices is certainly much greater.

New Demands on Government:
Building and Maintaining Institutions

Isaiah Berlin once observed, "Any study of society shows that every solution creates a new situation which breeds its own new needs and problems."[18] Welfare reform is no exception. The institutions of welfare now focus more on finding jobs for poor caregivers. Agencies are communicating new signals to families about their work obligations. The political popularity of the reforms, a growing economy, and ample federal funds have created unprecedented resources for childcare, employment, and other work-support services. Many states have also given local welfare agencies the flexibility and incentives to apply these signals and services to the diverse employment problems of a heterogeneous population of poor families.

It takes nothing away from these institutional changes to say that they are generating new questions and problems. The complexity, adaptiveness, and decentralized character of the new welfare constitute at least partial evidence that state and local administrative systems are changing more rapidly and profoundly than any other set of American public institutions. But welfare reforms are also challenging our governing institutions: by reducing the role of legislatures, they may narrow the range of political interests able to influence social programs; by making traditional forms of evaluation and analysis more difficult and less useful, policy debates may be less informed; and by focusing attention on aggregate effectiveness, less attention may be paid to individual rights.

How can these problems be addressed? Three directions seem promising: First, as argued above, there is a need to invest in welfare information and statistical systems that meet a much wider variety of management and political needs — that is, to create information systems that are almost as rich, as flexible, and as devolved as the new welfare systems themselves. Second, they suggest the need for considerable professionalism and sophistication among the people and organizations operating these programs. Returning to a highly regulated system entailing considerable oversight by central authorities may address some of the issues concerning clients' rights and program understanding and assessment, but that tactic may also ensure that local systems will never be particularly effective in adapting to local conditions. To work well, the new programs

187

require considerable trust between central authorities and local agents in their competence, and a mutual understanding of which factors are appropriate and inappropriate in making decisions and implementing processes that affect so many lives. This, to be sure, is a challenge itself, as there are no dominant professions in this policy area, and social work — the one profession that has been involved in welfare administration — has to date not adapted to the demands for more expertise in employment and jobs. Nonetheless, to the extent that front-line workers and local administrators need to balance so many values and interests in their day-to-day operations, reconciling these diverse concerns may require recruiting high-quality managers and workers with common beliefs about goals, values, and appropriate behavior.

Third, the issues also suggest the need for building new forms of political representation and strengthening older ones. In particular, there is a need to bring greater political representation or involvement down to the local level, where many of the critical decisions are made. In some places, that is happening. Florida has created new representative institutions in its local WAGES Coalitions, and though there are controversies over the composition of those boards, the basic idea of moving representation down to where the basic decisions and adaptations are being made is a promising one. Some form of political representation is also occurring as community organizations get more involved in promoting outreach among families in order to boost CHIP and Medicaid enrollments, and as local advocacy organizations perform their own assessments of the status of welfare leavers and of their problems in obtaining services. These activities may often be incomplete and unsystematic, but they may bring pressures to bear on local administrative systems to respond more systematically to a broad range of values and concerns in the community.

In many ways, these challenges are more manageable in the Midwest, not only because states in that region have more experience with welfare reform, but even more important, because they have more experience with governmental reform. Much more than the AFDC program, the new welfare, to work well, demands good government.[19] Many of the more complex structures and functions emerging in the midwestern states — such as the job centers and W-2 contracts with local providers in Wisconsin, the highly interactive relationships between state and county agencies in Ohio, and the growing cooperation between the welfare and workforce development bureaucracies in Michigan — are probably inoperable without a sophisticated and professional public workforce. A state ethos that values research and analysis in developing policies — an ethos that lies at the heart of the Progressive tradition and that is clearly evident in the extensive support for welfare policy research in Wisconsin and Minnesota — is also crucial. If welfare reforms in the Midwest are ultimately more effective in helping families achieve self-sufficiency and escape poverty, other states may need to learn about their systems of government as much as their specific innovations in social policy.

Endnotes

1   Albany, NY: Rockefeller Institute, 1999.

2   Bonney & Company, *The National Poll on Welfare Reform and Healthcare Reform: Results of a National Survey Regarding Devolution, Healthcare Reform and Welfare Reform Conducted for the W.K. Kellogg Foundation*, Virginia Beach, VA: Bonney & Company, January 13, 1999. See Table 2.

3   Janet Looney and Betty Jane Narver, "Meeting the Goals of Washington's Workfirst Program: Key Policy Changes," in *Managing Welfare Reform: Updates from Field Research in Five States*, edited by Thomas Gais (Albany, NY: Rockefeller Institute, 1999). A revised version of this volume, edited by Professor Sarah Liebschutz, will be released in the spring of 2000 by the Rockefeller Institute Press and distributed by the Brookings Institution Press.

4   On this two culture hypothesis, see the presentation by Professor Irene Lurie, "State Capacity Study: Implementing PRWORA at the Local Level," at Evaluating Welfare Reform, a conference sponsored by the Administration for Children and Families, Office of Planning, Research, and Evaluation, of the U.S. Department of Health and Human Services, Arlington, Virginia, May 12, 1999. The study is being conducted at the Rockefeller Institute with funds from the U.S. Department of Health and Human Services. The principal investigator is Professor Richard P. Nathan, and the two other senior investigators are Professors Norma Riccucci of SUNY-Albany and Marcia Meyers of Columbia University. For a discussion of agency cultures under AFDC, see Mary Jo Bane and David T. Ellwood, *Welfare Realities: From Rhetoric to Reform* (Cambridge, MA: Harvard University Press, 1994), pp. 15-19.

5   Term limits may, of course, contribute to legislative weakness, but though the limits have clearly affected the composition and leadership of legislatures, it is still too early to discern their consequences for the policymaking process. See Francis X. Clines, "Term Limits Bring Wholesale Change into Legislatures," *New York Times,* February 14, 2000.

6   For a discussion of the role of AFDC waiver evaluations in the formulation of state TANF programs, see Thomas Gais and Richard Nathan, "Learning, Emulation, and Adaptation in the American States: The Case of Welfare Reform," paper presented at the Annual Research Conference of the Association for Public Policy Analysis and Management, Washington, DC, November 1999.

7   Hans Both, et al., *New Hope for People with Low Incomes: Two-Year Results of a Program to Reduce Poverty and Reform Welfare,* New York: Manpower Demonstration Research Corporation, 1999.

8   Cynthia Miller, Virginia Knox, Patricia Auspos, Jo Anna Hunter-Manns, and Alan Orenstein, *Making Welfare Work and Work Pay: Implementation and 18-Month Impacts of the Minnesota Family Investment Program,* New York: Manpower Demonstration Research Corporation, 1997.

9   A critical factor might be, for example, whether states and localities have the capacity to understand how welfare applicants and recipients are proceeding through program processes — a capacity that may require (especially in large urban areas) management information systems that fit the new change-oriented welfare reforms. See, for example, Michael Wiseman, *A Management Information Model for New-Style Public Assistance,* Discussion Paper 99-10, Assessing the New Federalism Project, Washington, DC: Urban Institute, August 1999; Terrence Maxwell, *Information Federalism: History of Welfare Information Systems,* Working Paper, Albany, NY: Rockefeller Institute, 1999; and Nathan and Gais, *Implementing,* pp. 52-63.

10   Good waiver evaluations collect data on implementation, but they tend to view this component of the research simply as a check that the program "as enacted" was carried out. See, for example, Dan Bloom, Laura Melton, Charles Michalopoulos, Susan Schriver, and Johanna Walter, *Jobs First: Implementation and Early Impacts of Connecticut's Welfare Reform Initiative,* New York: Manpower Demonstration Research Corporation, February 2000.

11   The basic design of the TANF block grant creates an important source of program instability. By requiring states to meet a "maintenance-of-effort" requirement — a minimum amount of state spending in support of the goals of the Personal Responsibility Act — states are under pressure during periods of economic growth, when caseloads are down, to expand the range of services provided to families and individuals. This pressure may not exist in the same way during economic downturns.

12   For summaries of these studies, see Jack Tweedie, Dana Reichert, and Matt O'Connor, *Tracking Recipients After They Leave Welfare,* Washington, DC: National Conference of State Legislatures, July, 1999; U.S. General Accounting Office, *Welfare Reform: Information on Former Recipients' Status,* GAO/HEHS-99-48, Washington, DC: U.S. General Accounting Office, April 1999; Sarah Brauner and Pamela Loprest, "Where Are They Now? What States' Studies of People Who Left Welfare Tell Us," *New Federalism: Issues and Options for States,* Series A, No. A-32, May 1999.

13   On the importance of management information systems to satisfy some of these requirements, see note 10 above. As of early 2000, 1995 poverty data were the latest available for counties. See U.S. Census Bureau, "Small Area Income and Poverty Estimates: Tables for States and Counties by Income Year and Statistic," November 3, 1999 (last revised), http://www.census.gov/hhes/www/saipe/stcty/estimate.html. One of the

more encouraging developments is the expected full implementation of the American Community Survey (ACS) by the Census Bureau in 2003. The ACS "will provide estimates of demographic, housing, social, and economic characteristics every year for all states, as well as for all cities, counties, metropolitan areas, and population groups of 65,000 people or more." These data include poverty estimates. U.S. Census Bureau, "About the American Community Survey," http://www.census.gov/CMS/www/acs.htm.

14 See the *U.S. Code of Federal Regulations*, vol. 45, ch. II, secs. 205-206 (1997).

15 On food stamps, see U.S. General Accounting Office, *Food Stamp Program: Various Factors Have Led to Declining Participation*, GAO/RCED-99-185, Washington, DC: General Accounting Office, 1999. Estimates of the effects of welfare reform on food stamp caseloads may be found in Geoffrey Wallace and Rebecca M. Blank, "What Goes Up Must Come Down? Explaining Recent Changes in Public Assistance Caseloads," in *Economic Conditions and Welfare Reform,* ed. by Sheldon Danziger, Kalamazoo, MI: W.E. Upjohn Institute, 2000. On Medicaid, see Families USA Foundation, *Losing Health Insurance: The Unintended Consequences of Welfare Reform,* Washington, DC: Families USA Foundation, 1999; Marilyn R. Ellwood and Kimball Lewis, *On and Off Medicaid: Enrollment Patterns for California and Florida in 1995*, Occasional Paper Number 27, Washington, DC: Urban Institute, 1999; Leighton Ku and Brian Bruen, "The Continuing Decline in Medicaid Coverage," Number A-37, *New Federalism: Issues and Options for States*, Washington, DC: Urban Institute, 1999. On both programs, see Frank J. Thompson and Thomas L. Gais, "Federalism and the Safety Net: Delinkage and Participation Rates," unpublished manuscript, Albany, NY: Rockefeller Institute, 2000.

16 Robert E. Crew and Joe Eyerman, *Explaining Low Demand for Child Care Funds in Florida's Welfare Reform Program,* unpublished manuscript, Tallahassee, FL: Florida State University, 1999. This project was supported with funds from the Florida Department of Children and Families. In response to the question "Did you have an opportunity to meet with a child care counselor?" 29 percent of English-speaking respondents (persons who were receiving public assistance) said yes, while only 15 percent of Spanish-speaking respondents said yes.

17 John Stuart Hall and Gerald J. Kubiak, "Arizona's Welfare Reform Experience," *Rockefeller Report*, Albany, NY: Rockefeller Institute, November 1999.

18 Isaiah Berlin, *The Proper Study of Mankind: An Anthology of Essays*, New York: Farrar, Straus and Giroux, 1998, p. 12.

19 I am thankful to Professor Lawrence Mead of New York University for this point.

About the Authors

Charles Adams is a professor in the School of Public Policy and Management at Ohio State University and a faculty associate with the John Glenn Institute of Public Service and Public Policy. In addition to his research on the design and implementation of welfare reform in Ohio, his current research includes a project in the Eastern Cape Province of South Africa on local democratic reforms and the role of community partnership grantmaking in promoting citizen participation in newly created local democratic structures. He is also working in conjunction with the OECD Fiscal Decentralization Initiative on the design of a framework for gauging citizen trust and satisfaction in matters of local democratic governance in Central and Eastern Europe.

Thomas Gais is director of the Federalism Research Group of the Nelson A. Rockefeller Institute of Government of the State University of New York. He is co-principal investigator and project director of the Institute's Capacity Study, a multi-year research project on the changing institutions and management systems at the state and local levels in welfare, Medicaid, and workforce development. His previous work dealt with issues of institutional change and reform, including campaign finance reform, constitutional change in the states, and interest group mobilization in American national politics. Gais received his Ph.D. from the Department of Political Science at the University of Michigan-Ann Arbor.

Thomas Kaplan is senior scientist at the Institute for Research on Poverty, University of Wisconsin-Madison, where he also teaches courses in social policy and public assistance management at the La Follette Institute of Public Affairs. He holds a Ph.D. in history from the University of Wisconsin-Madison and served for 15 years in Wisconsin state government, including as deputy budget director, planning director, and director of Medicaid HMO programs in the state Department of Health and Social Services. His current research and publications concern welfare reform and the use of administrative data in program evaluation.

Jocelyn M. Johnston is assistant professor of public administration at the University of Kansas, where she teaches public finance and intergovernmental relations. Her research focuses on intergovernmental programs and policy regarding state-local issues such as county finance, government contracting, property tax administration, and school finance. She is co-editor, with H. George Frederickson, of *Public Management Reform and Innovation: Research, Theory and Application*. Her publications have appeared in *Public Administration Review, Public Budgeting and Finance, Journal of Public Administration Research and Theory, Publius: The Journal of Federalism, State and Local Government Review*, and *Journal of Health and Social Policy*.

Kara Lindaman is a graduate student in political science at the University of Kansas. Her studies focus on public administration and American politics. Her research interests include social programs and policy at the subnational level.

Thomas F. Luce, Jr. is an Assistant Professor of Public Affairs and Planning at the Hubert H. Humphrey Institute of Public Affairs, University of Minnesota. His research and teaching focus on state and local public finance, metropolitan development and policy, urban affairs, and intergovernmental relations. His most recent work includes research on Minnesota state budget policies for a multistate study of state fiscal policies in the 1990's, tax-base sharing in the Twin Cities and several other metropolitan areas, the potential impact of congestion pricing on employment subcenters in the Twin Cities metropolitan area, welfare reform in Pennsylvania and Minnesota, and various other aspects of economic development patterns in American metropolitan areas. Before joining the Humphrey Institute, Luce taught at Pennsylvania State University and was Associate Director of the Wharton Economic Monitoring Project at the University of Pennsylvania (where he co-authored three books on the Philadelphia area economy and public sector). He received an M.S. in Economics from Birkbeck College, University of London and a Ph.D. in Public Policy Analysis from the University of Pennsylvania.

Carol S. Weissert is associate professor of political science and director of the Program in Public Policy and Administration at Michigan State University. She holds a Ph.D. in political science from the University of North Carolina-Chapel Hill. She has recently published articles in *Journal of Politics, Health Affairs, Publius: The Journal of Federalism, Journal of Health, Politics, Policy and Law,* and *Administration and Society,* and is co-author of *Governing Health: The Politics of Health Policy* (1996). She serves as co-editor of the annual review edition of *Publius: The Journal of Federalism.* Her current research and publications concern intergovernmental issues in welfare reform and health policy.

Miriam Wilson is an instructor in Public Administration at Ohio University. Her research interests include welfare reform and development of alternative delivery systems for governmental programs. Her public-sector experience includes managing the Ohio Office of Labor-Management Cooperation and working for the U.S. Senate on the staff of Senator John Glenn. Wilson has a masters degree in human resource management and is a doctoral candidate in public policy and management from Ohio State University.

Index

in Michigan, 141, 150-151,
162
in Minnesota, 132
in Ohio, 32
in Wisconsin, 79, 83, 84-85,
87, 90-91

See also Job services; Job
training
W-2. *See* Wisconsin welfare reform